# Life Skills for Teenage Boys

*Essential Keys to Developing Self-Confidence, Overcoming Challenges, and Unlocking a World of Possibilities*

# Table of Contents

# Introduction Letter to Parents

Dear Parents and Guardians,

As you embark on the exhilarating journey of parenthood, you'll face challenges at each stage of your child's growth. The transition to teenage years – the reason you're reading *this* book – is extraordinary, marked by significant emotional, intellectual, and physical changes. It's time for your son to become independent, focus on self-discovery, and thrive, but it can also be challenging for both parents and teens to navigate effectively. As their primary caregiver, it's important to recognize this transformative phase in your son's life and equip him with the tools and guidance necessary to navigate this phase of his life successfully.

In this book, he will learn about the physical and emotional changes that come with puberty and how to cultivate self-awareness and build a strong sense of identity. He'll also learn about vital concepts like socialization and setting objectives; he'll also develop skills like emotional resilience.

He'll gain a deeper understanding of anxiety and stress, helping him develop emotional resilience, enabling him to handle peer conflicts better, and making him confident enough to reach out for help when necessary. From money management to life skills, survival skills, and much more, this book will be the best guide for your son at this age.

Every topic discussed here is approached with the utmost sensitivity, care, and respect, creating a safe and nurturing space where he can better understand himself and the world around him. Despite having all this knowledge, he'll still need your support and guidance. Therefore, actively engage and be a supportive figure in his life. Your involvement, understanding, and support will be pivotal in his journey toward becoming a confident, responsible, and well-rounded individual.

# Introduction Letter to Children

Dear Reader,

Your teenage years are an extraordinary time in your life, filled with change, growth, and discoveries that will shape the adult you'll become. This book isn't just any book. It's your trusted companion on this incredible journey of personal development and self-discovery. It's here to let you know that you are seen, valued, and celebrated for who you are right now.

The purpose of this book is simple but profound: to equip you with the life skills and knowledge you need to survive and thrive during your teenage years. These skills are the stepping stones that will guide you toward a future where you can achieve your dreams and aspirations.

Throughout these pages, you'll become familiar with topics like understanding your changing body, managing your emotions, building healthy relationships, and making smart financial choices. The most important part, the one you need to keep in mind right away, is that your thoughts, questions, and experiences matter. Think of this book as a conversation. You're encouraged to participate and engage with it actively.

Remember, the skills and knowledge you gain from this book aren't just useful in your teenage years. You'll soon find out that they will set you on a path to success in the future. So, start learning, embrace the process, and grow into the amazing young adult you're destined to be.

# Section 1: Puberty: Taking Care of Yourself

First things first, understanding the physical and emotional changes you're going through is crucial. Puberty is a huge change your body goes through as you go from childhood to teenagehood. Think of it as nature's way of preparing you for the future.

Puberty is a huge change your body goes through as you go from childhood to teenagehood.
*https://pixabay.com/photos/change-new-beginning-risk-road-3256330/*

## What Happens in Puberty?

### Hormonal Changes

The human body produces hormones that act as tiny messengers. They can control several functions and induce changes in your body. When you hit puberty, your body starts producing a hormone called testosterone, which marks the start of the changes you'll experience.

### Physical Changes

Soon after puberty starts, your body will start experiencing significant changes. You will start getting taller, your muscles will become stronger, and even your voice will change. You'll also notice hair growing under your arms, on your face, and in your pubic area.

Your private parts will also experience some changes. Your testicles (will get bigger, and you will start having erections. All of this is a natural part of growing up. Some boys can even grow a full beard shortly after puberty starts.

### Fluctuating Emotions

You might also notice your emotions being all over the place. You might feel really happy one moment, and you could be mad or sad the next. This is because your brain is growing and changing, too.

# What's Exactly Happening Inside?

All of these changes are happening because of the hormone testosterone. Think of it like the captain of a ship, guiding your body through these changes. It tells it to grow, make sperm (the tiny cells needed for making babies), grow taller and stronger, and much more.

# When Does Puberty Start?

Puberty usually starts between ages 9 and 14, but it's different for everyone. Your body has its own timetable, so don't worry if it doesn't happen at the same time as your friends.

# What Can You Do?

**Stay Healthy:** Eating balanced meals and staying active helps your body grow strong during this time. To follow a healthy routine, avoid eating processed foods and limit your visits to your favorite fast food chain, as they are loaded with unhealthy carbs and fats.

**Embrace Change:** Puberty can feel a bit strange sometimes, but it's all part of growing up. Embrace the changes, and remember, you're becoming a young adult.

**Asking Questions:** If you have questions about puberty, you can ask trusted adults (like your parents, a teacher, or a doctor) to help you find the right path and understand what's going on.

**Patience:** Think of puberty like a video game. You start at level one and must play through all the levels to finish the game. It takes time, practice, and patience to level up and become the hero of your own story.

**Responsible Behavior:** Being responsible is part of being an adult. For example, when using the internet, be responsible with it. For example, you wouldn't give your keys to someone you don't trust, so be careful with your online personal information!

You're not alone on this adventure. Every man goes through puberty, and there are lots of people who can help you understand what's happening. So, stay curious and keep learning about this phase of your life.

# Physical Self-Care

Physical self-care is paramount for teenagers as it plays a pivotal role in their overall health and well-being during a crucial phase of growth and development. Engaging in regular exercise and maintaining proper hygiene not only fosters physical health but also promotes mental and emotional balance. By adopting healthy eating habits, getting enough sleep, and practicing self-care routines, you can boost your energy levels, improve your mood, and enhance your concentration, all of which are vital for academic success and personal growth.

Physical self-care instills lifelong habits that help prevent chronic illnesses and set the foundation for healthy adulthood. Learning to prioritize physical well-being equips you with the tools you need to thrive and navigate the challenges of adolescence with both resilience and vitality.

# Hygiene and Grooming

**Bathing:** Take showers or baths regularly, especially after physical activities. Use soap to clean your body thoroughly, including your armpits, feet, and private parts. Scrub gently to remove dirt and sweat. That will keep you feeling fresh and prevent body odor.

**Brushing Teeth:** Ensure you're brushing your teeth at least twice daily. Use toothpaste with fluoride in it and a soft-bristled brush, and do this for around 2 minutes. Don't forget to floss every day to remove food particles.

**Washing Hands:** Wash your hands with soap and warm water for at least 20 seconds before eating, after using the bathroom, and when visibly dirty. Washing your hands regularly prevents the spread of germs and illnesses.

**Haircare:** Comb or brush your hair regularly to keep it neat and prevent tangles. Washing it every couple of days or as needed helps remove dirt and excess oil. Always use a shampoo suitable for your hair type.

**Nail Care:** Keep your fingernails and toenails clean and trimmed. Use a nail clipper or file to keep them tidy. Clean under your nails to prevent dirt buildup.

## Skincare

**Sunscreen:** Apply sunscreen with at least SPF 30 when you go outside, especially in the sun. This is important because you need that protective barrier to keep UV rays that can be damaging to your skin at bay. If you live in a place with a lot of sun, go for one with a higher SPF number than 30. However, it's recommended to consult a dermatologist before doing that for teens with sensitive skin or skin conditions.

**Moisturize:** Use a gentle moisturizer to keep your skin hydrated, especially in winter. Dry skin can become itchy and uncomfortable when it's not hydrated properly.

## Healthy Sleeping Habits

**Set a Routine:** Try to go to bed and wake up at the same time every day, even on weekends. This regulates your body's internal clock and improves the quality of your sleep. Try to go to sleep between 9 pm to 10 pm and get at least 8 hours of sleep.

**Create a Comfortable Sleep Environment:** Make your bedroom a sleep-friendly place. Keep it dark, quiet, and cool. Use comfortable pillows and a mattress that provides good support.

## Sleep Hygiene

The quality of your entire day hinges on your sleep. During the day, avoid daytime naps. Also, increasing outdoor activities has been shown to improve sleep. Once in bed, relax, let go of troubling thoughts, and avoid doing anything stimulating.

**Limit Screen Time:** Try to avoid any kind of screen exposure for at least 1 hour before going to bed. The blue light they emit can interfere with your ability to fall asleep. Most phones, tablets, and smart TVs have an option to decrease blue light emission. Use that if you must use one of your devices for school or something important. Remember that even with that feature on, it will affect your sleep routine and strain your eyes with prolonged use.

## Healthy Eating

**Balanced Meals:** Aim to eat a variety of foods from different food groups. Include fruits, vegetables, grains, protein sources (lean meat, fish, beans, and nuts), and dairy products. This ensures you get a mix of all the essential nutrients.

**Drink Water:** Stay hydrated by drinking plenty of water throughout the day. Water helps your body function properly and can prevent dehydration.

Stay hydrated by drinking plenty of water throughout the day.
*https://unsplash.com/photos/person-holding-clear-drinking-glass-PCpoG06fcUI*

**Limit Sugary Treats:** While enjoying sweets occasionally is okay, try not to overdo it. Too much sugar can be harmful to your teeth and overall health. Sugary snacks will affect your memory and learning and lead to obesity. Opt for healthier snacks like fruits or yogurt.

Taking care of your body through physical self-care routines is like maintaining a well-oiled machine. It ensures your body functions at its best, keeps you feeling good, and sets the foundation for a healthy future. By practicing these habits, you invest in your well-being and overall health. Don't forget that no one is perfect, and learning about new things takes time. If you are confused at any point or can't figure out the next step, contact family members or teachers for guidance.

# Basics of Sexual Education

Sexual education is a crucial component of understanding human relationships and our bodies. When exploring these essential aspects of life, it's important to recognize that knowledge empowers individuals to make informed decisions and fosters a safe, respectful, and responsible approach to one's sexuality.

Your body is incredible, and part of growing up involves understanding it better. Boys and girls have different body parts, each with their own functions.

### Development of Sexual Characteristics

During puberty, boys develop male sexual characteristics, such as facial hair, a deeper voice, and growth in the genital area. Girls experience changes, too, like breast development and the start of menstruation.

### Managing Sexual Thoughts and Feelings

**Normal Feelings:** It's normal to start having sexual thoughts and feelings during adolescence. These feelings are part of growing up and exploring your own body.

**Respect and Privacy:** Remember that your body is private, and so are your feelings. It's important to respect your own boundaries and the boundaries of others.

**Communication:** If you have questions or feel confused, it's okay to talk to someone you trust, like a parent, guardian, teacher, or healthcare professional. They can provide guidance and answer your questions.

### The Concept of Consent

Consent is giving permission or agreement. In intimate relationships, it means that both people agree to do something willingly and without pressure.

**Mutual Agreement:** Consent must be mutual, meaning both people say "yes" freely and enthusiastically.

**Communication:** Open and honest communication is key. It's important to talk with your partner about your desires and boundaries and to listen to theirs.

**Boundaries:** Everyone has personal boundaries, and it's crucial to respect them. If someone says "no" or changes their mind, you should stop and respect their decision immediately.

**Age and Consent:** Understand that the age of consent varies by location and can impact who can legally engage in sexual activities. Be aware of the laws in your area.

**Consent Is Ongoing:** Consent isn't a one-time thing. It is ongoing throughout both the act itself and the entire relationship. You can change your mind at any point, and it's important to communicate that.

**Respect and Trust:** Respect your partner's decisions and trust them to respect yours. This creates a safe and healthy environment for both of you.

**No Pressure:** Never pressure or manipulate someone into doing something they're uncomfortable with. Remember: consent should always be *freely given – not coerced or forced in any way.*

**Consent Education:** Educate yourself and your partner about consent. The more you know, the better you can ensure that both of you have a safe and positive experience.

Understanding your body, managing your feelings, and practicing consent are all part of growing up. These principles guide healthy relationships and ensure you and your partner are comfortable, safe, and respected.

# The Basics of Mental Health

Mental health is just as crucial as physical health, and caring for your mind is part of leading a fulfilling and balanced life. Understanding the basics of mental health and self-care empowers you to manage stress, build resilience, and maintain emotional well-being. In this section, you'll explore fundamental skills and techniques to help you nurture your mental health, from practicing mindfulness to setting clear boundaries and seeking support when needed.

Mental health is just as crucial as physical health, and caring for your mind is part of leading a fulfilling and balanced life.

### The Connection between Self-Care and Mental Health

Emotional and mental self-care for teens encompasses a range of practices and skills that promote well-being and resilience. It involves recognizing and understanding one's emotions, managing stress, and seeking support when needed. Importantly, it's about prioritizing one's mental and emotional health just as much as physical health. This is particularly crucial for teenagers, as adolescence is a time of significant change, growth, and increased emotional complexity.

Developing a foundation of emotional and mental self-care during this period helps you navigate the challenges of school, relationships, and self-discovery and equips you with essential life skills for the future. It fosters self-awareness, emotional regulation, and healthy coping mechanisms, allowing you to build a strong foundation for mental well-being that can benefit you throughout your life.

The relationship between self-care and mental health is akin to the connection between a well-tended garden and the flowers that bloom within it. Just as a gardener tends to the soil, waters the plants, and provides the right conditions for growth, self-care is the nurturing process that supports your mental health. When you prioritize self-care, you are essentially tending to the garden of your mind, ensuring it remains fertile, resilient, and capable of flourishing.

Engaging in self-care practices, such as managing stress, practicing mindfulness, and setting boundaries, equips you with the tools to navigate life's challenges, maintain emotional balance, and foster a positive sense of well-being. In essence, self-care is a vital cornerstone of mental health, and by embracing it, you empower yourself to lead a healthier and happier life.

### Mindfulness and Meditation

**Deep Breathing:** Take slow, deep breaths to calm your mind and reduce stress. Breathe in slowly through your nose, hold for a few seconds, and then exhale through your mouth.

**Body Scan:** Close your eyes and focus your attention on each part of your body, starting from your toes and moving up to your head. This helps you become more aware of physical sensations and relaxes tense muscles.

### Establishing Clear Personal Boundaries

**Learn to Say "No":** It's okay to say "no" when someone asks you to do something that makes you uncomfortable.

**Voice Your Needs:** Calmly and assertively communicate your needs and expectations. Let people know what you're comfortable with and what you're not.

### Emotional Regulation

**Identify Feelings:** Learn to recognize and name your emotions. Sometimes, acknowledging your feelings can help you manage them better. After identifying the emotion, try keeping your head clear of unnecessary thoughts and shifting your focus towards managing your emotions.

**Journaling:** Write down your thoughts and feelings in a journal. This can help you process emotions and gain insight into what's going on in your mind.

### Stress Management

**Exercise:** Engage in physical activity you enjoy, whether it's sports, dancing, or even just a relaxing walk. Exercise releases endorphins, which are natural mood lifters.

**Hobbies and Relaxation:** Dedicate time to activities you love, like reading, drawing, or listening to music. These hobbies can provide a break from stress and recharge your mind.

### Self-Compassion

**Positive Self-Talk:** Practice speaking to yourself kindly and encouragingly. Treat yourself as you would treat a good friend. When facing an emotionally challenging situation, avoid blaming yourself and instead focus on facing these challenges and finding a resolution.

**Self-Care Rituals:** Establish self-care routines, such as taking relaxing baths, enjoying your favorite tea, or taking short breaks to recharge during the day.

### Goal Setting and Planning

**Set Achievable Goals:** Break your goals into smaller, manageable steps. This makes tracking your progress and feeling a sense of accomplishment easier. You can try the SMART goal strategy, which is easy to incorporate into your daily routine and makes goals more manageable.

**Time Management:** Use tools like calendars or planners to organize your tasks and prioritize what's most important to you. You can even use time management apps on your computer or smartphone to make this much easier.

# Seeking Support

**Talk to People You Trust:** Reach out to friends, family members, or a counselor when you're feeling overwhelmed or need someone to talk to. Sharing your thoughts and feelings can provide relief.

**Support Groups:** Joining a support group related to a particular challenge you're facing can help you connect with others who share similar experiences.

# Gratitude Practice

**Daily Gratitude:** Take a moment each day to reflect on things you're grateful for. It can be as simple as appreciating a beautiful sunset or a kind gesture from someone.

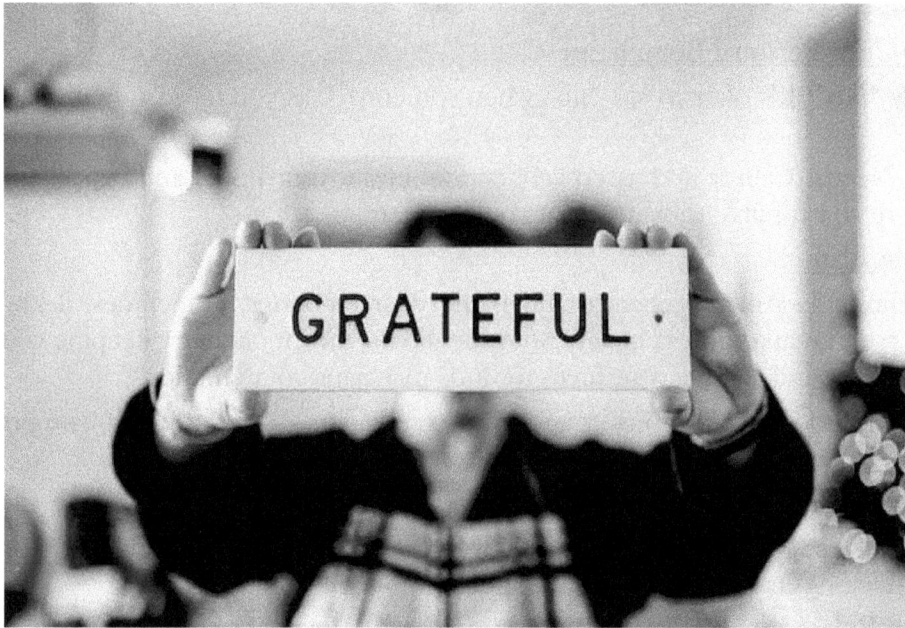

Take a moment each day to reflect on things you're grateful for.
https://unsplash.com/photos/person-holding-white-and-black-i-love-you-print-card-fs_10Xqlc90

# Stress Reduction Techniques

**Progressive Muscle Relaxation:** Tense up and then relax different muscle groups, starting from your toes and moving up to your head. This helps release physical tension. It's an advanced technique and may need guidance from a certified integrative health specialist.

**Visualization:** Close your eyes and imagine a peaceful place, like a beach or a forest. Visualizing a calming scene can reduce stress and anxiety.

# Time for Yourself

**Me Time:** Dedicate some time each day or week to do something just for yourself. Whether it's reading a book, taking a walk, or enjoying a hobby, this time should be all about you.

Remember, mental and emotional self-care is an ongoing practice. Mix and match these techniques to create a self-care routine that works best for you. Prioritize your well-being, and don't hesitate to seek professional help if you ever feel overwhelmed or need additional support.

# Section 2: Discovering Yourself

In the grand adventure of life, one of the most thrilling journeys a teenage boy can embark on is self-discovery. Understanding who you are, what you stand for, and what makes you unique is the cornerstone of personal growth and development. It's about uncovering your strengths, understanding your weaknesses, and aligning your actions with your values.

In the grand adventure of life, one of the most thrilling journeys a teenage boy can embark on is self-discovery.

*Photo by Mounir Abdi on Unsplash* *https://unsplash.com/photos/a-person-standing-on-a-cliff-d1-urKRfkKc*

This chapter will set the stage for an exploration that will take you to exciting places within yourself. In this section, you'll learn an array of skills and concepts designed to help you uncover the extraordinary person you are and have the potential to become. Whether you're dealing with low self-esteem, struggling with peer pressure, or simply looking to enhance your self-awareness, the skills you're about to explore will empower you to take charge of your life.

# Skill 1: Self-Reflection and Introspection

In today's fast-paced, constantly connected world, pausing and looking inward is a precious skill. Self-reflection is like holding up a mirror to your thoughts, emotions, and experiences.

### How to Start Self-Reflecting

Getting started with self-reflection might seem daunting, but it's simpler than you think. Find a quiet and comfortable space free from distractions. This could be your room, a park, or even your favorite quiet corner in a library. Make a habit of carving out some time for this practice, whether a few minutes before bed or during a quiet morning.

Now, simply breathe and let your mind wander. Focus on your recent experiences, interactions, and emotions. Ask yourself questions like:

- What made me happy today?
- What challenged me today?
- How did I react to certain situations?
- What did I learn today?
- What could I have done better?

As you regularly engage in self-reflection, you'll gain a deeper connection with your inner self. You'll become more attuned to your thoughts and emotions and discover patterns that can lead to personal growth.

### Gaining Insight into Your Thoughts and Feelings

Self-reflection isn't just about asking questions. It's about actively exploring your thoughts and emotions. It's the process of becoming a mindful observer of your inner world. When you're feeling a strong emotion, like anger or happiness, take a moment to dissect it. Ask yourself why you're feeling that way. Is there a specific trigger or a cumulative effect of various experiences?

Recognizing the origins of your emotions can empower you to respond to them in healthier ways. For instance, if you know you tend to get anxious in certain situations, you can develop strategies to manage that anxiety effectively.

### Journaling for Self-Reflection

Journaling provides a tangible record of your thoughts, emotions, and experiences. It's a safe space to express yourself without judgment. You can jot down your thoughts, challenges, triumphs, and dreams. The benefits of journaling for self-reflection include:

- Tracking your personal growth over time.
- Uncovering recurring themes or issues in your life.
- Reducing stress by expressing your feelings on paper.
- Organizing your thoughts and ideas.

• Setting and reviewing personal goals.

Make a habit of regularly writing in your journal, whether daily, weekly – or whenever you feel the need.

# Skill 2: Exploring Interests and Passions

Discovering and nurturing your passions can be a powerful catalyst for self-awareness. When you engage with activities you are genuinely interested in, you learn more about your preferences, values, and what makes your heart sing.

Pursuing your passions can lead to a sense of purpose and fulfillment. It can ignite your motivation and drive, helping you set meaningful life goals. Identifying your interests is not just about what you like to do in your free time. It's about understanding who you are and what you want to achieve.

Discovering and nurturing your passions can be a powerful catalyst for self-awareness.
*https://www.pexels.com/photo/selective-focus-photography-of-paintbrush-near-paint-pallet-1047540/*

## Tips for Trying New Things

While identifying your existing interests is crucial, being open to trying new things is equally important. Stepping out of your comfort zone can be a remarkable way to uncover hidden passions. Here are some tips to consider:

- **Be Open-Minded:** Embrace new experiences with an open heart and mind. Don't dismiss an activity before you've given it a fair chance.
- **Experiment:** Don't be afraid to experiment with various activities. You might be surprised by what captivates you.
- **Join Clubs and Groups:** Seek out clubs or groups related to various interests. This is a fantastic way to meet people who share your potential passions and gain insights into different activities.
- **Learn from Others:** Talk to people who are passionate about their interests. Their enthusiasm can be contagious, and you may find their passion resonates with you.

### Exploring New Hobbies and Interests

To ignite your curiosity, here are examples of activities to explore:

- **Sports:** Try different sports, whether soccer, swimming, or martial arts. Physical activities are great for both fitness and social interaction.
- **Art and Creativity:** Experiment with drawing, painting, music, or creative writing. These activities allow you to express yourself and develop your creative skills.
- **Nature and Outdoors:** Explore activities like hiking, camping, or gardening. Connecting with nature can be a transformative experience.
- **Science and Technology:** Dive into the world of science or technology through robotics, coding, or scientific experiments. The possibilities are endless.

### Setting Personal Goals

As you explore new interests and passions, consider setting personal goals. Goals give your exploration a purpose and direction. They help you measure your progress and motivate you to keep going. For instance, if you discover a passion for painting, set a goal to complete a certain number of paintings in a month or participate in an art exhibition. These goals enhance your commitment and provide a sense of achievement and satisfaction.

## Skill 3: Identifying Personal Strengths and Weaknesses

Understanding yourself involves recognizing what you enjoy, what you excel at, and where you have room to grow. Identifying your personal strengths and weaknesses is a key element in the journey of self-discovery. To recognize your strengths, consider:

- **Self-Reflection:** Reflect on your life experiences. What tasks or activities have you consistently excelled at? These are likely your strengths.
- **Feedback from Others:** Sometimes, those around you see your strengths more clearly than you do. Ask friends, family, and mentors for their perspectives on your strengths.
- **Trying New Things:** Experiment with different activities and hobbies. You'll quickly discover what comes naturally to you.

### Areas for Improvement

Your weaknesses are not limitations; they are areas for growth and development. To acknowledge and work on your weaknesses constructively, consider the following:

- **Self-Awareness:** Reflect on your life experiences and consider your challenges. What areas do you struggle with consistently?
- **Seeking Feedback:** As with strengths, ask for feedback from trusted individuals. They can offer insight into where you could improve.
- **Goal-Setting:** Set goals that challenge you in the areas you want to improve. Setting goals can drive your growth, whether in public speaking, time management, or patience.
- **Learning and Practice:** Invest time in learning and practice to develop the skills you need to improve. If, for example, you struggle with public speaking, take a course or join a club to practice regularly.

### The Power of Self-Assessment

Self-assessment is the ability to evaluate your strengths and weaknesses objectively. This self-awareness empowers you to make informed decisions and set realistic goals. It involves reflecting on your past experiences, your performance in various situations, and the feedback you've received from others. It's a continuous process that helps you better understand yourself and make choices that align with your personal growth.

# Skill 4: Clarifying Values and Beliefs

Your values and beliefs make up the compass that guides you in life. They shape your decisions, actions, and priorities. When your actions align with your values, you experience a profound sense of purpose and authenticity. Here's why they matter:

- **Authenticity:** Values reflect your true self. You are your most authentic self when you align with your values.
- **Clarity:** Values provide clarity in decision-making. They serve as a reliable reference point for choosing your path.
- **Resilience:** Knowing your values can help you stand firm in facing challenges and adversity. Your values are your moral compass.
- **Fulfillment:** Living in alignment with your values leads to a sense of fulfillment and contentment.

### How to Uncover Personal Values

Identifying your core values requires introspection and self-awareness. Here's a step-by-step guide to help you uncover your values:

- **Self-Reflection:** Take time to reflect on experiences that have been meaningful in your life. What made them significant, and why?
- **Identify Influences:** Think about the people who have significantly impacted you. What values do they represent, and which ones resonate with you?
- **Prioritize:** List the values that come to mind and prioritize them. What values are non-negotiable, and which ones hold the most weight for you?
- **Refine:** Continuously refine your list of values as you gain a deeper understanding of yourself. Your values may evolve over time.

### Making Value-Based Decisions

Once you've clarified your values, making value-based decisions becomes more natural. Consider these principles:

- **Prioritization:** When faced with a choice, evaluate how it aligns with your values. Choose the option that resonates most with your core principles.
- **Alignment with Goals:** Make sure that your values align with your long-term goals. This synergy will drive you towards a more fulfilling life.
- **Integrity:** Uphold your values, even when it's challenging. Consistency between your beliefs and actions is a sign of integrity.

• **Consider Consequences:** Think about the potential consequences of your decisions on your values and the people around you.

# Skill 5: Emotional Intelligence

Emotional intelligence is a skill that many people should have. It allows you to become in tune with not only your feelings and emotions but also those surrounding you. It's important to understand and manage emotions more skillfully, and it's critical to have this skill because it definitely influences and affects your relationships with your friends, peers, colleagues, and family members. Check the following strategies below to help you handle your emotions in a much healthier manner:

• **Self-Awareness:** Begin by recognizing your emotions as they arise. Label them and understand their triggers. This self-awareness is the first step in managing your emotions.

• **Emotion Regulation:** Learn how to control intense emotions using relaxation techniques, mindfulness, or deep breathing. This prevents impulsive or harmful reactions.

• **Healthy Expression:** Express your feelings honestly and constructively. Avoid bottling up your emotions, but also steer clear of explosive outbursts.

Express your feelings honestly and constructively.
https://unsplash.com/photos/shallow-focus-photo-of-man-looking-at-trees-Gee1LDFJRQc

• **Seek Support:** Don't hesitate to talk to a trusted friend, family member, or counselor when your emotions become overwhelming. They can provide valuable guidance and support.

### Conflict Resolution Skills

Conflict is a natural part of relationships, but how you handle it matters. The following are some tools for resolving conflicts peacefully and constructively:

- **Active Listening:** In a conflict, actively listen to the other person's perspective without interrupting. Understand their point of view before responding.
- **Use "I" Statements:** Express your feelings and thoughts using "I" statements like "I feel" or "I think" instead of making accusatory statements.
- **Seek Common Ground:** Look for areas of agreement or compromise. Finding common ground can resolve conflicts more effectively.
- **Stay Calm:** Avoid escalating conflicts with anger or aggression. Stay calm and collected to create a safe space for resolution.

## Skill 6: Boosting Confidence and Self-Image

Confidence is the foundation for building a fulfilling and successful life. It's not about being arrogant. It's about having faith in your abilities and understanding your intrinsic worth. The following are tips for enhancing your self-confidence and self-belief:

- **Set and Achieve Small Goals:** Start with achievable goals and celebrate successes. Each small win boosts your confidence for more significant challenges.
- **Positive Self-Talk:** Monitor your inner dialogue. Replace self-criticism with self-encouragement. Challenge negative thoughts and focus on your strengths.
- **Body Language:** Practice confident body language by maintaining good posture, making eye contact, and speaking clearly. It makes you appear more confident and affects how you feel about yourself.
- **Learn and Improve:** Continuous learning and self-improvement build competence, which, in turn, boosts your confidence.

### The Role of Positive Self-Image

Self-image is how you perceive yourself and the value you place on your abilities and qualities. It influences your behavior, choices, and interactions with others.

- **Influences Behavior:** Your self-image shapes your behavior. If you see yourself as capable and valuable, you're more likely to take on challenges and enthusiastically pursue your goals.
- **Impacts Perceptions:** Your self-image affects how others perceive you. When you project a positive self-image, it encourages respect and admiration from others.
- **Affects Well-Being:** A positive self-image leads to higher self-esteem and better mental health. It reduces stress and anxiety and increases overall life satisfaction.

## Skill 7: Effective Communication

Effective communication can transform your personal and professional relationships. It encompasses a wide range of skills, including active listening, assertiveness, conflict resolution, and public speaking, collectively shaping your ability to express yourself and connect with others.

### Active Listening

Active listening is the foundation of effective communication. To become a better listener and understand others, consider these techniques:

- **Maintain Eye Contact:** Show the speaker you're engaged and attentive by maintaining eye contact.
- **Avoid Interrupting:** Resist the urge to interrupt or formulate a response while the other person is speaking. Let them finish before you respond.
- **Paraphrase and Clarify:** Summarize what you've heard to show that you were paying attention and to guarantee you understood correctly. Ask questions for clarification if needed.
- **Nonverbal Cues:** Pay attention to the speaker's body language and emotions. They can convey a lot about what they're saying.

### Public Speaking and Presentation Skills

Effective public speaking and presentation skills are valuable in various aspects of life, from giving a speech in school to leading a meeting at work. Here are some tips to help you confidently express your ideas in front of others:

- **Prepare and Practice:** Thoroughly prepare your speech or presentation and practice it multiple times. Rehearsal builds confidence.
- **Engage Your Audience:** Keep your audience engaged through storytelling, interactive elements, or thought-provoking questions.
- **Body Language:** Pay attention to your body language. Maintain good posture, use gestures, and make eye contact.
- **Breathing and Relaxation:** Practice deep breathing to manage nervousness.
- **Visual Aids:** If you're using visual aids, make sure they enhance your message without overwhelming the audience.

# Skill 8: Time Management and Goal Setting

Effective time management and goal setting are essential life skills that can pave the way for personal and academic success. These skills help you make the most out of your time, set meaningful goals, and achieve your aspirations. Here are strategies for efficiently organizing and utilizing your time:

- **Create a Schedule:** Develop a daily or weekly schedule and allocate specific time slots for different activities, including studying, extracurriculars, relaxation, and social interactions.
- **Avoid Procrastination:** Recognize the signs of procrastination and employ strategies like the Pomodoro Technique (work for 25 minutes, then take a 5-minute break) to stay productive.
- **Use Technology Wisely:** Leverage digital tools and apps like calendars and to-do lists to stay organized and set reminders.

### Goal Setting for Success

Goal setting is a powerful technique for achieving both short-term and long-term aspirations. Here's how to effectively set and pursue your goals:

- **Be Specific:** Define your goals clearly and concisely, and avoid vague objectives. Use the SMART criteria (Specific, Measurable, Achievable, Relevant, Time-bound) instead.

---

- **Break Goals Down:** Divide larger goals into smaller, manageable steps. This makes the journey more manageable and achievable.
- **Visualize Success:** Establish a mental image of any result you wish to have. Visualization can enhance your level of commitment to your goals and boost motivation.
- **Track Progress:** Monitor your progress regularly. Adjust your approach as needed, and celebrate all achievements along the way.
- **Stay Accountable:** To hold yourself accountable, share your goals with someone you trust, like a friend or family member.

# Skill 9: Financial Literacy

Financial literacy is all about being savvy with your money. It spans topics like budgeting, saving, investing, and understanding financial systems. Having a good grasp of these concepts is essential for your financial well-being:

- **Money Management:** Financial literacy teaches you how to manage your finances and make responsible financial choices effectively.
- **Security:** It provides the knowledge and tools needed to protect your financial security and plan for unexpected expenses.
- **Long-Term Goals:** It helps you set and achieve long-term financial goals, such as buying a car or a home or funding your education.
- **Investment:** It equips you with the skills to make smart investment decisions, potentially increasing your wealth over time.

### Budgeting and Saving

Budgeting and saving are fundamental skills in financial literacy. They are key to managing your finances, ensuring financial stability, and achieving your financial goals:

Budgeting and saving are fundamental skills in financial literacy.
*https://www.pexels.com/photo/person-putting-coin-in-a-piggy-bank-1602726/*

- **Budgeting:** Create a budget that outlines your income and expenses. This helps you see where your money goes and make informed decisions about your spending.
- **Saving Money:** Develop a habit of saving a portion of your income. Even small savings can add up over time and provide a financial safety net.
- **Emergency Fund:** Save for emergencies by setting aside money for unexpected expenses.

# Skill 10: Resilience and Stress Management

Resilience and stress management are invaluable life skills that help you navigate challenges and maintain your mental and emotional well-being. These skills empower you to bounce back from setbacks, manage stress effectively, and seek support when needed. Here are strategies for building resilience:

- **Positive Mindset:** Cultivate a positive outlook by focusing on your strengths and past successes. Optimism can help you face difficulties with resilience.
- **Problem-Solving:** Develop effective problem-solving skills. Break challenges into smaller, manageable parts and work toward solutions.
- **Emotional Regulation:** Learn to manage your emotions. Techniques like deep breathing, mindfulness, and meditation can help you stay calm during tough times.
- **Seek Support:** Reach out to trusted friends, family, or mentors for guidance and emotional support. You don't have to face challenges alone.

### Coping with Stress

Stress is a natural part of life, but how you manage it can greatly impact your well-being. Here are techniques for managing it and maintaining your mental health:

- **Recognize Stressors:** Understanding what's causing you this amount of stress is the first step in managing it efficiently. Identify the sources of your stress.
- **Healthy Lifestyle:** Prioritize self-care by exercising regularly, maintaining a balanced diet, and getting enough sleep. A healthy body is more resilient to stress.
- **Time Management:** Efficiently manage your time to reduce the pressure of looming deadlines. Use time management techniques to stay organized.
- **Hobbies and Activities:** Engage in activities you enjoy, such as sports, art, music, or reading, to give yourself an escape from stressors.

# Section 3: Socialize like a Pro

Once you discover yourself and become independent, you may begin to wonder why you need to socialize with others. You are happy and content in your own space. What's the point of mingling with other people? Ask yourself this instead. How long are you going to thrive without company? How long will you survive? At the moment, you may feel like you don't need anyone, but a few years down the line, your perception is bound to change.

How long will you keep discovering yourself? There will come a time when you will feel the need to discover new people, their passions, habits, joys, sorrows, past, present, future, and so much more. To do that, you should develop your social skills.

There will come a time when you will feel the need to discover new people, their passions, habits, joys, sorrows, past, present, future, and so much more.

*https://unsplash.com/photos/low-angle-photography-of-two-men-playing-beside-two-women-UmV2wr-Vbq8*

# Social Skills

Social skills are the abilities that allow you to interact and communicate with people. Imagine that a new student is sitting beside your desk at school. How will you start a conversation with them? If you are moderately social, you may begin with a simple "Hi." Extroverts will compliment them by saying: "Hey, that's one great pair of shoes!" If you are an introvert, initiating a conversation, no matter how badly you want to, won't even cross your mind. That's primarily due to a lack of social skills.

Do you tend to talk for a long time without giving the other person a chance to talk? For instance, while narrating an incident, do you keep droning on and on without seeing whether the listener is actually listening?

Do you often criticize your peers? Do you keep interrupting them instead of listening to what they have to say? These are the most common mistakes that people make while interacting with others. Here are a few tips to avoid that:

- Observe the listener as you talk. Do they seem interested? If not, change the topic.
- Listen to yourself. Is what you're saying interesting to you, or do you feel like you're talking just for the sake of it?
- Stop judging people. They may like something you don't, but it doesn't give you the right to judge them.
- As you judge people less and less, you will automatically learn not to criticize them.
- When someone is talking, let them finish. Don't interrupt. If you feel like you have something to contribute, make a mental note of it. Say it only when they have stopped talking.

# Social Dynamics

Social dynamics refer to how something causes social states to change. Take the friendship between two people as an example. When two friends develop romantic feelings for each other, you can say that their social dynamics have been affected.

You may only have one best friend at one point in your life. At another point, you may be in a group of best friends. How one group of people interacts with another falls under social dynamics. For instance, are you a group of high school seniors whom others have recently started looking up to?

One major benefit is being able to identify the social dynamics among different groups of people. It enables you to recognize an unhealthy, negatively inclined group. Before joining a particular group at your school, observe how other groups perceive them. Do they often generate a negative vibe while interacting with other groups? Do they stir up disharmony and violence wherever they go? That's definitely a group with unhealthy social dynamics, and you would be better off staying away from them.

# Effective Communication

Imagine you want to borrow a book from a student in your class. You know that you simply need to ask, "Hey, may I borrow that book?" and thank them when they lend it to you. However, when you approach them, are you left tongue-tied? When you muster the courage, do you say something in broken sentences, like, "May I...book?" With effective communication, you will be able to say exactly what's on your mind without breaking a sweat.

- **Talk to Yourself**

There's nothing wrong with talking to yourself to develop your communication skills. You're most likely already talking to yourself all the time in your mind. It's time to do it out loud. Stand in front of a mirror and say whatever is on your mind. Start by saying, "Hey, I feel good today," and think as if the person in the mirror asks, "Why are you feeling good?" Respond with the reasons and continue the conversation.

- **Talk to a Family Member**

One of the reasons many people lack communication skills is not talking to their parents as much as they should. When they return home from school, ask them, "Hey, Dad, how was your day?" or, "Hey, Mom, did you do anything new today?" Find a way to start the conversation. The rest will follow.

- **Take the Initiative**

When you want to communicate with someone new, don't wait for them to approach you. Take the initiative and approach them yourself. You don't have to think up a witty line to make friends at your age. Just go to them and say, "Hi!" Tell them why you wanted to talk to them, something like, "I wanted to talk to you about our homework."

# Active Listening

Listening actively means showing that you are listening to the speaker. It doesn't mean simply hearing the person. You acknowledge what they are saying and respond accordingly. It is one of the most important social skills to learn.

- **Focus on the Conversation**

You should focus on what's being said. Every little detail counts. Pay attention so you can consciously form an appropriate response.

- **Maintain Casual Eye Contact**

Don't bore into their eyes or give them a thousand-yard stare. Casually maintain eye contact. Look away from time to time as if you are trying to understand what they are saying. Don't look at your phone or the wall. They may think that you want to end the conversation.

- **Don't Interrupt**

This cannot be stressed enough. Never interrupt the speaker unless absolutely necessary. Let them finish talking before correcting them, even if they said something wrong.

- **Don't Jump to Conclusions**

Did they say or do something you don't approve of? Don't jump to conclusions. They probably haven't mentioned the context just yet. Listen to everything they have to say before judging their behavior. If you still don't approve, say it to their face, not behind their back. Assure them you understand where they're coming from unless it's really bad.

- **Interrupt Only to Ask Questions**

Did you not understand something they said? Only then should you politely interrupt and ask them about it. Otherwise, you won't understand the rest of the conversation. For example, they may have said a word you're not familiar with. Ask them what it means. It also shows that you are listening and are interested in the conversation.

- **State Your Opinions, Don't Stress Them**

When people share their problems with you, they are not looking for opinions or possible solutions. More often than not, they only want you to listen. So, if you have nothing but opinions or solutions to respond with, stay quiet. Hear them out. When they are done talking, ask them politely, "Would you like to hear what I honestly think?" Give your opinions only if they agree. Don't impose or stress them.

# Body Language and Nonverbal Communication

Did you know that more than 60% of human communication is nonverbal? The way you move, your posture and body language, and even the number of times you blink says a lot about you. To the observant individual, your nonverbal cues will provide great insight into your personality and thinking.

While you may not want to seem like an open book, you can use nonverbal cues to communicate more effectively. You can stress your point with your hands, show your frustrations with your arms, demonstrate your anger with your fists and legs, or convey your sorrow with your face.

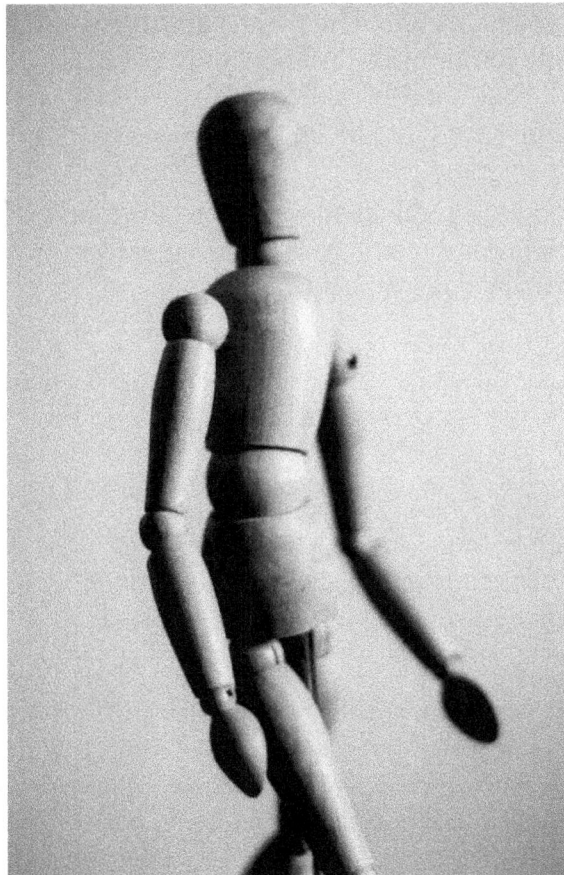

Most human communication is non-verbal.
https://unsplash.com/photos/colse-up-photo-of-brown-wooden-doll-_Zd6COnH5E8

- **Facial Expressions**

Your face is the most important nonverbal communicator during a conversation. While talking, other body parts are easy to miss, but your face stands out because that is where the listener is focused on. Your facial expressions can convey almost all the known emotions.

- **Gestures**

Have you noticed that many people tend to gesticulate while talking? They wave their arms, keep pointing nowhere in particular, slap their thighs, you name it. You may also be making one gesture or another while speaking. You may not even have realized it yet! Gestures often accentuate what you say, showing you're passionate about the topic.

- **Other Body Movements**

When talking to someone, you should stand or sit facing them (at an angle will also work). Are you talking while walking? Walk side by side. Nod or shake your head often (as the situation demands) to show that you are listening. Are they talking about a sad incident? Hold their hand or place your arm on their shoulder. Are they sharing a happy incident with you? Give a full, warm smile from time to time.

# Build and Maintain Meaningful Friendships

This is the most useful skill you can learn. The friendships that you forge at your age will last for a lifetime. Apart from being with you through thick and thin and helping you live life in general, your friends will develop your confidence and provide a safe space to share your daily joys and sorrows. While bullying isn't as common these days, friends will also protect you from any instances that crop up.

Ideally, making a friend comes as naturally to you as breathing, but you may find it difficult due to your low self-esteem or trauma from the past. Without going into its psychological depths, here are a few tips to help you build and maintain meaningful friendships.

- **Make an Approach**

Don't wait for them to come to you. If you are interested in being friends with someone, don't hesitate to make an approach. Just go over to their desk and say, "Hi." What's the worst that could happen?

- **Grab an Opportunity**

Schools provide a number of opportunities for students to build friendships. Ask about your homework. Help them understand a complex study concept. Build a rapport during leisure activities. Discuss a chapter or a topic while hanging out outside of school.

- **Be More Approachable**

When other students pass you in the corridors, make friendly eye contact and give them a smile. When you join a study club or a project group, introduce yourself and try to remember everyone's names. Acknowledge their presence with a nod and a smile. Look the speaker in the eye and give occasional nods of understanding. When asked to speak, try to make eye contact with everyone.

- **Respond Enthusiastically**

Did one of your peers approach you between classes? Respond positively. Say "Hi" back, ask them how you could help them, and so on.

Once you have built a friendship, you need to maintain it. That is probably the hardest thing to do in the initial stages. Talk to them when you both have free time. Don't bother them when they are busy studying or doing homework. Try to be there whenever they need you. Stand by their side when the situation demands. Celebrate their joys and be with them through their grief. Keep in mind that for them to be a good friend, they need to reciprocate all of those things.

# Approaching a Romantic Interest

Romance in children is not as common as in adults, but you often experience your first love at this age. Don't hesitate to act on that feeling. Just tell them how you feel. You don't have to be creative, but if you are, your chances of getting a positive response will soar.

### • Develop a Friendship

Did you know that most romantic relationships start from friendship? Use the tips mentioned in the previous section to develop a friendship with your potential romantic interest. Over time, if they begin to like it, it may just blossom into a romance.

### • Start with a Compliment

Tell them straight up what you find attractive about them. It can be their hair, eyes, clothes, or any accessories.

### • Start with a Witty Remark

Intelligence is as attractive as physical appearance. Compliment them in a unique way. Think up a line that is witty and interesting, something that will catch their attention.

# Building Confidence and Self-Esteem

While friendships improve your confidence, you need to possess it to start a friendship in the first place. Confidence comes from believing in yourself and your skills. Self-esteem is how you see and appreciate yourself. Essentially, confidence and self-esteem go hand in hand. The higher your self-esteem, the more confident you will be, and vice versa.

- Know that making mistakes is human nature. Don't see a mistake as a blow to your self-esteem. Learn from it and move on.
- Failures are a part of life. Don't let them get you down. A string of failures is often followed by several successes. Look forward to those successes instead of brooding on the former.
- Be self-compassionate. Regardless of your failures and successes, treat yourself with the same level of love and care.
- Your relationships with other people determine your level of self-confidence. Hanging out with positive people will boost your self-esteem, whereas being with a negative group will lower it.
- Talk to yourself as a mentor talks to a mentee. Say inspiring, confidence-building quotes out loud every morning.
- Indulge in self-affirmation. Tell yourself time and again how worthy you are. See your own value in your mind's eye. Self-affirmation is critical, especially when you are feeling down.
- Embrace a growth mindset. Try to figure out what went wrong and learn from it whenever you fail. Don't let that failure pull you down. Assure yourself that success is just around the corner. All you have to do is keep walking and growing to achieve it someday.
- Focus more on the positives in your life. Don't dwell on the negatives.

# Learning to Empathize

Empathizing is understanding what others are feeling. It's the act of resonating with their emotions and showing that you care. Usually, you empathize when someone is going through a tragedy. Here are a few tips to become more empathetic.

- You may never have felt the kind of tragedy your friend is going through, but you can always connect with the emotion. Let them know you understand how they are feeling.
- Try to remember something similar that has happened in your life and share your story.
- Listen to what they have to say. Stay quiet if you cannot say something that will help the situation.
- Use your imagination. Put yourself in their shoes. How would you feel if it had happened to you? Once you get the answer, react accordingly.

# Conflict Resolution

Conflicts can occur between different groups of people or between people from the same group. It could be anything from a misunderstanding during a project to a full-blown fight while playing a game. You need to be level-headed and mentally present to resolve conflicts.

- Don't deny that it's a conflict; accept the fact.
- Proceed to listen to both parties; use your active listening skills.
- Think of a mutually beneficial solution.
- If you cannot do that, simply agree to disagree.

# Leadership and Mentoring

An aspect of building a thriving social life is becoming a leader. A leader doesn't always inspire revolutions and organize protests. You can learn to be a leader in little things, like your group's social dynamic or your team's project, or you can lead yourself! It's the attitude that matters.

An aspect of building a thriving social life is becoming a leader.
*https://unsplash.com/photos/scrabbled-scrabble-tiles-with-words-on-them-EkyuhD7uwSM*

- Explore yourself and recognize your values. What do you stand for? Practice not to give up on your values and morals.
- Show respect to gain respect.
- Don't hesitate to help others in need. It can be as simple as helping them move into your dorm room.
- Select a good role model and try to be like them without losing yourself. Be a role model to others.
- Become a trustworthy member of your group.
- Applaud the achievements of others.

You should always begin by looking within yourself. Know your strengths and weaknesses when it comes to socializing. Work on your weaknesses until they become your strengths. Otherwise, simply accept your weaknesses and move on. Only then could you acquire the confidence to socialize like a pro.

# Section 4: Universal Skills

There are certain skills you gain throughout life that can be applied in multiple different contexts. A foundation of useful mental tools can allow you to overcome any obstacles the world throws at you. As a teen, you are filled with potential. Your youthful energy can be channeled to take your life in any direction. However, you need to remember that as you age, the impact of your decisions could have life-long consequences. To jump on the train heading toward greatness, you must be on the platform of critical thinking, time management, creativity, empathy, and respect while traveling on the railroad of your purpose.

Repetition breeds habit, so these universal skills must constantly be implemented in all areas of your life. Applying the principles outlined in this chapter with clinical precision can put you on the fast track to manifesting a bright future socially, financially, physically, and mentally. There will inevitably be roadblocks and hurdles that spring up along the way, but with the right tools, you will power through. Take your time to develop this toolset so you can start seeing the innumerable benefits at school, home, and work. Consciously applying yourself with disciplined effort will open portals to unleash the map that guides you to your vision. Taking some time daily to work on getting better at the various techniques listed throughout this chapter will profoundly impact how you perceive the world so that you can have the perfect mindset to achieve your dreams.

A foundation of useful mental tools can allow you to overcome any obstacles the world throws at you.
*https://www.pexels.com/photo/background-blank-business-craft-301703/*

# Critical Thinking

Due to your environment and upbringing, many of your thought patterns are automatic. People do not often evaluate their thoughts to test their alignment with reality. Critical thinking aims to get a more accurate view of the world and to embrace thought forms that result in the best outcomes for your life. Critical thinking is the process of questioning your views and opinions and the external information you receive to weigh whether they are true or misguided. A few major institutions affect human opinion, including the government, religion, society, education, and family. As you grow, you begin questioning some of the views that were thought to be by way of all these institutions. Critical thinking is the mechanism you can use to measure which views you want to keep and what you want to discard. Furthermore, it can help you determine which new opinions and perspectives you are introduced to are worth embracing.

### Activity 1: Questioning Yourself

The best way to begin practicing critical thinking is by yourself.

Can you think of some opinions you have accepted as true without even questioning them? For example, you may believe some gender stereotypes.

- Do you recall when you started believing this?
- Why do you hold this view?
- What data is available to support your current view?
- Is it possible that you are wrong about this opinion?
- If this opinion is wrong or based on inaccurate information, how can you determine what a more correct view is?
- Can you think of something you believed when you were younger but no longer believe now?
- Why did you stop believing that?

The key to critical thinking is always to question everything. Never accept any claim at face value. Many people become trapped in unfavorable situations because they never question their reality. Growth can only come from evolving your views over time.

### Activity 2: The Trolley Problem

Sometimes, there is no right or wrong answer. Your opinion will be based on what you value and what has been taught to you. A great way to explore your values and demonstrate how complicated truth claims can be is the trolley problem.

There is a train traveling on a railway that splits into two tracks. You have control of a lever that directs where the train goes. If you do not pull the lever, the train will go on to kill five people. If you pull the lever, it will kill only one person. Will you pull the lever to save the five people and kill one, or will you just stand there and allow it to kill five?

Most people at this point say they will pull the lever to save five and kill one, but the problem can get more complicated.

- What if the five people are all serial killers, and the single person is an innocent child?
- What if the single person is a family member you care about, and the other five are complete strangers?

Can you see how there are many different variables to consider? There are many grey areas in life, so you always need to explore all the options before making a decision.

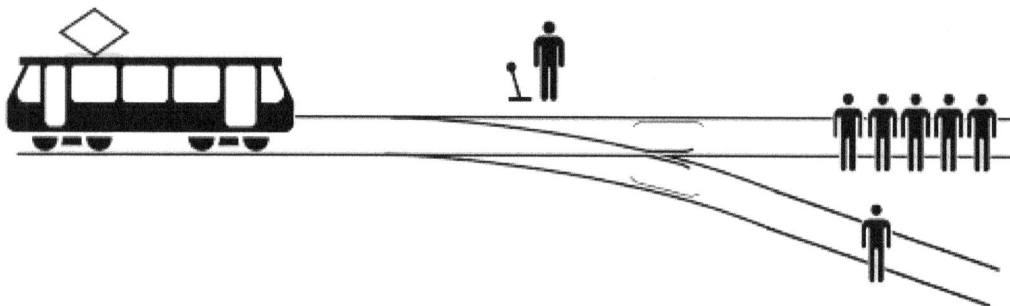

# Time Management and Organization

Managing your time well and organizing your life are key indicators of whether you will achieve success. When you waste your time or spend it recklessly, it is almost certain that you will increase your stress levels and lessen your ability to cope. Think about a school assignment. If you work on it a little bit every day from when it was given, it will be a far less stressful experience than if you were to try to complete the assignment the night before the due date.

### Activity 3: Crafting a Daily Schedule.

Planning your day is central to managing your time well. The most successful people in the world have their day scheduled down to the hour and sometimes even to the minute. A popular saying goes, "Failing to plan is to plan to fail." Time is limited. You only have 24 hours in the day to work with. You sleep for 8 of those hours, which means that you really only have 16 hours to be productive.

Write a list of the daily tasks you must complete each day. Include grooming, chores, school work, after-school activities, and time for recreation. Once you have written everything down, calculate how long each task will take to complete.

Once you have worked out how long each activity takes, make a daily schedule for Monday to Friday, and then make a separate one for the weekend since you do not have school to attend on Saturday and Sunday.

Write down which activities you will do at what time. Stick to your schedule to build a routine that will slowly transform into a habit.

### Activity 4: Understanding How to Live in The Moment.

Procrastination is one of the biggest dream killers. To be successful, you must understand the importance of finishing a task as soon as possible. At the beginning of the day, write down a to-do list of everything you want to achieve. When you get home from school, start working on them immediately. If you put things off until later, you may never get it done.

# Problem-Solving

The journey of life will not always be smooth. Sometimes, you'll be paddling along on calm, shiny seas, and other times, you will be bashed against violent waves looking to topple over your boat. When unfavorable situations inevitably come along, you must be prepared to deal with them decisively.

To effectively solve problems, you must be able to step back, look at the bigger picture, and zoom into the finer details. This complete analysis will help you make the right decisions to achieve your desired outcomes. With a clear and calculated mental state, you can pick apart your issues surgically. Some problems can be anticipated, while others will blindside you. Accepting the reality that issues can arise at any point gives you the perseverance to brush off the spiderweb of problems you find yourself facing.

### Activity 5: Step to Problem Solving

Solving a problem must be approached systematically, *or you will be overwhelmed.* The following steps are how you can start to solve problems.

**Step 1: Define the Problem.** Before tackling any issue, you first need to define it. Ask yourself the following questions:

- What is the problem?
- When did it develop?
- How did you become aware of it?
- Is there any extra information you need to obtain about the issue?

**Step 2: Develop Goals for Solving the Problem.** Think about how your situation will look once your problem is solved. Visualize yourself after dealing with this issue. Write down short, medium, and long-term goals related to your problem.

**Step 3: Identify the Cause of Your Problem.** Sometimes, the issues you experience are a result of something else. For example, you may be failing a subject at school, but the cause of your failure may be an emotional issue you are having because of something at home. To stop failing, you need to mend the emotional issue you have.

**Step 4: Develop a Plan of Action.** Break your problem down into smaller, manageable chunks. For example, you may have failed a subject in school. Instead of tackling it as one giant issue, break it down into steps you can take to make sure you do not fail. Maybe start by spending one hour per day studying the subject. Which section did you have problems with? You could spend more time on those topics. Be detailed in the description of what steps you will take to remedy the adverse situation.

**Step 5: Evaluation.** Once you have implemented your plan of action, you must assess what is working and what is not. Only then can you make adjustments to your plan to ensure constant improvement.

### Activity 6: Building Resilience

Problems in life are unavoidable. You cannot allow the problems that arise to knock you over. You need to develop reliance, which is the ability to continue pushing forward despite the challenges. A great way to build resilience is by doing something difficult daily, like exercising. Set some time aside to work out before you go to school. Pushing yourself can make you more mentally capable when problems knock at your door.

# Creativity and Innovation

Creativity and innovation are what drive modern society. A research study conducted in 2014 with 242 participants concluded that there is a strong correlation between creativity and academic success (Nami et al., 2014). Creativity can help you with problem-solving so you can innovate new solutions by looking at a situation from different angles. Being creative can be innate, but it is also a skill that can be nurtured over time. Everyone is creative in their own way, so it is up to you to discover how you can express yours in a way that will benefit you.

Creativity and innovation are what drive modern society.
https://www.pexels.com/photo/teenage-boy-writing-on-a-chalkboard-6256241/

## Activity 7: Learning New Things

Challenge yourself to learn something new out of your comfort zone every week. The internet has given you the ability to look up anything in an instant. YouTube offers free courses on multiple subjects. Search for something you do not see yourself doing, like drawing, painting, or sewing. Creativity is thinking outside of the box or even destroying the box completely. To be creative, you constantly have to flex your creativity muscles. Diving into new avenues of expressing yourself can build up parts of your mind that you never thought you'd use.

## Activity 8: Journaling

Outside forces influence creativity, but it is generated from within. What inspires you may be mundane to the next person because people's minds are so individualized. Writing in a journal can grow your creativity, especially if you get fancy with how you write. Create some songs or put together poems about your feelings and how your day went. It is amazing how something as simple as that can allow you to explore yourself. From creativity comes innovation. That new world-changing idea might be hidden just below the surface, so keep digging.

# Empathy and Respect

Humans are sharing limited space and resources on the planet. They have to work together to prosper. Empathy and respect can help you better collaborate with others in school, work, or social environments. When you show respect and compassion, most of the time, you will receive the same treatment in return. People get down on their luck and complain about how the world treats them, but it is rare to reflect on how you treat others. Respect and empathy are birthed by the understanding that people are all going through something and have reasons to act how they do. Having a little understanding of others can help you build the connections you need to prosper.

You contribute to making the world more pleasant. Everybody is having a hard time. When someone shows you kindness, it helps lift the burdens of life off your shoulders. In this selfish age, people tend to be harsh and are more than willing to step on others to get to the top. The problem with this crab-in-a-bucket mentality is that when you pull people down, others will also drag you lower. Being uplifting, respectful, and empathetic creates a chain of positivity that extends further than you think it would. One kind act could encourage someone to push through hardships. When you are not around, you never know what someone is going through, so kindness is always the better option.

### Activity 9: Understanding Others

Empathy and respect come from your ability to understand other people and imagine yourself in their shoes. It is easy to become selfish and only think about how the world is treating you, but all the humans on the planet have a deeply profound life experience, just like you are.

- Think about the last fight you had with your parents. How did you feel, and what was it about?
- Now, put yourself in their shoes. How do you think you made them feel?
- Why do you think they reacted the way they did?
- How does the way your parents grew up differ from yours?
- How do the differences in perception, age, and culture affect your and your parents' relationship?

Sometimes, taking the time to think about a situation from someone else's point of view, even if you do not agree with them, can help you gain respect for them.

# Purpose

Your purpose is the main guiding principle in life. Every decision that you make should be to fulfill your life's purpose. The meaning of life is not the same for all people. You are responsible for finding and pursuing your purpose so that it can act as the compass that points you where you should go instead of wandering through life.

There are very few things sadder than a purposeless life. Your purpose makes your life worth living and is something personal that no one else, even your parents, can define for you. The beauty of having an immovable is that you have the power to create meaning. The most fulfilling undertaking is the internal process of reframing the mundane into something magical.

## Activity 10: Defining Your Purpose

Some people never find the purpose that gives their life meaning, and it often has disastrous results. You are still young. Now is the perfect time to try on many hats to see which one fits. There are some key questions you should ask when defining your purpose.

- What do you value? You may value family, money, or your religion. The things you hold dearest to your heart are good indicators of your purpose.

- Where do you envision yourself in the future?

- What makes you happy, and what makes you sad?

- What activity could you do every day for hours without it feeling like work?

Write a story about your life. Think about events in the past that shaped how you think today. What in the present moment means the most to you? Write in detail the future you see for yourself. Take your time and think about it deeply. This exercise could guide you to find your inner drive and purpose.

# Section 5: Common Struggles and How to Deal With Them!

As you explore yourself in a diverse world, you will discover tons of conflicting ideas and ways of doing things. People's ideas always clash with each other, creating societal chaos. When you navigate the world, you will encounter uncontrollable barriers on your chosen path. Your struggles shape who you are. You can either grow from them or allow them to influence your vision. No one will tell you that life is easy. A big part of the human experience is continuous struggle. Nothing worth having is effortless. The road to all goals requires the conquering of internal and external dragons. Fortunately, your struggles are not unique, so you can use a blueprint of principles to overcome them.

Whether it's peer pressure, bullying, stress, or conflict, you have the power to make the changes needed to come out on top. Undeniably, it takes a mountain of work to get through the storms ripping apart the sails of your life, but with some guidance and assistance, you can build the resilience needed to keep pushing forward. The combination of establishing your boundaries, developing healthy coping mechanisms, regulating your emotions, being mindful, and strategic planning is the formula that will propel you quickly out of adversity and into the stratosphere. With perseverance and the right mindset, you can manage all the common struggles thrown at you throughout your teenage years and into adulthood.

## Peer Pressure

Society requires cooperation. Many of your most basic needs are tied to working together with others. Humans are completely reliant on one another. By cooperating in a group, individuals influence and adapt to each other. Through these social interactions, peer pressure emerges. Many people speak about peer pressure as if it is a bad thing, but it is just a natural consequence of being a person. Peer pressure could either have positive or negative outcomes. You need to understand the phenomenon of peer pressure and manage it in a way that promotes positivity in your life.

Society requires cooperation.
https://www.pexels.com/photo/three-young-hikers-looking-at-map-5622100/

## Activity 1: How to Handle Peer Pressure

Peer pressure is the process of adapting one's behavior out of the desire to fit in. The urge to fit in is sown deeply into the DNA of humans because people survive in groups.

Write down a few occasions where you did something you were uncomfortable with because your friends or people your age were doing it.

- What were the consequences of taking these actions?
- Write down how peer pressure can be positive and negative.

Peer pressure can not truly be avoided; it can only be managed. One of the key ways you can use it to your advantage is by joining groups or making friends with people that align with your values.

- Write down a list of your interests.
- Write down 10 goals you would like to achieve in the next five years.
- What kind of friends must you make to help you achieve these goals?
- Where can you find friends with interests similar to yours?

By thinking about where you would like to be in the future and what your interests are, you can decide which kinds of friends you want to make and, just as importantly, what activities you should say no to. Being aware of yourself and your desires can positively shape your decisions.

# Bullying

Many factors contribute to bullying. Some people bully others for attention, while others may be experiencing issues of abuse at home. Even though bullies often need help, nothing justifies treating people horribly. Bullying is not always physical. It can also be emotional, psychological, social, or verbal. Purposefully taking action to harm someone in any way is bullying.

### Activity 2: Steps to Take When Being Bullied

Here are some actions you can take to stop people from bullying you and others around you:

- Communicate with adults around you. Often, adults will not be aware of bullying or the new forms of harassment people experience. For example, cyberbullying is something that older generations may not be familiar with. Interventions and processes can be created to prevent bullying by keeping authority figures informed.

- Encourage forming groups among your peers where you can come together against unacceptable behavior. Bullies thrive in dividing and conquering. If a large group unites to stand against them, you can easily stand up to them.

- Set clear boundaries for yourself. Do not laugh along when you feel attacked, bullied, harassed, or uncomfortable. Verbally and sternly state what you will and will not accept, and attach consequences to your boundaries. For example, you can say, "I do not like being called that name. If you do not stop it, I will no longer be friends with you."

- If the bullying becomes violent, inform the relevant authorities. You cannot allow your safety and well-being to be threatened.

Remember that just because you are being treated terribly, it does not mean you can treat others the same way. The worst thing you can do when you are bullied is to inflict the same kind of torture on others.

# Embracing Change

Change can be very destabilizing if you do not have the necessary tools to deal with the shifts time brings. It is commonly said that the only constant in life is change. This saying exists for a good reason. Life never stagnates. New developments in society, school, family, and many other variables that make up the compilation of your life are constantly moving in waves of high and low points. Gaining the skills to ride these waves allows you to flow through adversity and enjoy the pleasures of life consciously with the awareness that will let you thrive.

### Psychological and Physical Changes

You are in a transitionary period between being a child and an adult. Many mental, physical, and social changes will occur as you go through puberty and gain the consciousness that allows you to take on more responsibility and accountability. Physical and hormonal transitions will change the way you interact with society and how people interact with you. The experiences you have as a teen will profoundly impact how you behave as an adult. Your identity is unfolding as you settle into who you are. Embrace this bumpy ride of change. Resisting change is futile because it is simply unavoidable. Brace yourself for impact and allow changes to mold you into a better person.

As you grow, you learn more and have more experiences. Your lessons, trials, conflicts, and victories affect your perception of the world. Imagine meeting your parents when they were your age.

You would be surprised by how they viewed reality compared to their current perceptions! Some changes are small and almost unnoticeable, but along the way, you will meet huge changes that redefine deeply held truths you once embraced wholeheartedly. These psychological shifts can bring about mental distress, anxiety, and sometimes even depression. Therefore, you must be in tune with your mental health, especially in times of change. Physical illness is easy to spot, but mental health issues can be hidden even from the individual experiencing them. Since change can easily influence your mental health, it is important to take steps to check on yourself.

### Activity 3: Mental Health Check

You can do the following exercise to check your mental health when you are going through a big or radical change. Even positive changes can be distressing, so this activity is relevant for any big shifts in your life.

You must be in tune with your mental health, especially in times of change.
https://pixabay.com/photos/mental-health-wooden-tiles-2019924/

Write down in-depth answers to all these questions when you experience significant changes in your life.

- What is the change you are experiencing?
- How does this change make you feel?
- What is the worst possible outcome?
- What will you do if this worst-case scenario occurs?
- What is the best possible outcome of this change?
- What will you do if the best-case scenario occurs?
- How will this change impact your life?
- Who or what can help you navigate this change?

# Emotional Regulation

You may have intense emotional peaks and valleys as you go through puberty. It is good to have emotions, but you cannot allow yourself to be controlled by them. Your emotions are valid. Emotional regulation is not the same thing as suppression. Negative feelings often indicate that something is wrong with your perceptions, behaviors, or environment. Avoiding or suppressing your negative feelings may provide temporary comfort, but in the long run, it does not address the underlying issues that have caused them in the first place. The only way to healthily regulate your emotions is by understanding them and working through them with mindful awareness.

### Activity 4: Emotional Regulation Techniques

Managing your emotions starts with being aware of them and able to identify and label your feelings. You are in a much better position to analyze the way you feel. Once your feelings are analyzed, you are better positioned to craft a plan to move forward and address the root of the negative emotions before having an outburst that can damage relationships.

You cannot choose your emotions, but you have control over how you respond to a triggering situation. When a situation induces negative feelings, you can follow these steps to manage your emotions:

- Take a deep breath. It may help to walk away for a bit if it is a heated situation.
- Feel your emotions. Do not try to suppress or deny what you are feeling.
- Think about the causes of the emotion and why you may feel that way.
- Communicate your feelings. People are unique, so what makes you feel angry or sad is not necessarily the same for the next person. You should speak openly about how you feel so people know how to treat you in various scenarios.
- Think deeply about the action you can take to create your desired outcome. Once you have slowed down, you can assess which actions to take instead of becoming a victim to your emotions and causing unnecessary havoc.

### Activity 5: Journaling

Processing how you feel can take some time. Journaling is an amazing way to slow down your thoughts enough so you can register exactly how you feel and why. Get a journal or notebook. Keep it next to your bed. When you wake up in the morning, write down how you feel, your expectations for the day, and any dreams you may have had. Before you go to sleep, write down how your day went. When writing about your day, focus on how you felt and what caused those emotions to arise. Journaling can be surprisingly insightful and help you be more emotionally aware.

### Activity 6: Mindfulness

Sometimes, it is difficult to recognize exactly how you feel or to put a word on an emotion. A mindful body scan can help you connect with your emotions and identify your feelings better. Lay or sit in a comfortable position. Take a few deep breaths and bring your awareness to your feet. Slowly shift your awareness up through your body toward your knees, then your stomach, all the way up through to your head. Pay attention to any discomfort in your body, like tenseness in your shoulders or stiffness in your back. Are there any emotions attached to your discomfort? Describe these feelings by how they feel in your body. This exercise can help you identify when negative emotions develop and will allow you to know how you experience negativity.

### Seeking Help

Negative emotions can sometimes become so intense that members of your support system, like your family and friends, do not know how to help you. People go through all kinds of emotions, and there will be high and low points. However, if you feel like you are constantly stuck at a low point, you may need to seek out professional help. You can speak to your school or your parents to start the process of finding you suitable mental health care. This professional support may be able to provide you with tools that your parents or peers may be ill-equipped for.

# Conflict Resolution

Conflict cannot be avoided. There is no one on the planet that you will agree with 100% of the time. Maintaining and building strong relationships requires you to be able to resolve conflicts. Trying to run from conflicts will make you a pushover that gets taken advantage of, and being too confrontational will cause your relationships to be strained. Finding a balance between asserting yourself and being willing to compromise is the sweet spot of dealing with the many conflicts that arise in life.

### Peer Conflicts

Peer relationships are some of people's most important bonds in life. Your peer group fulfills many of your social needs. Life can be difficult without people around your age with similar interests to interact with. As people get to know each other, they will inevitably cross some lines or disagree in some way. With life now having an extra digital layer, conflicts can follow you around even when you are not directly in someone's presence. Forming relationships with peers is complicated. You must decide which battles are worth fighting and what you can let go of to maintain a relationship.

### Parental Conflicts

Fighting with your parents is a bit different than fighting with your friends. Your parents are in a position of authority over you as your legal guardians and caregivers. As you begin forming your perceptions and opinions as an autonomous person, it is normal to have conflict with your parents. Being open and communicative can help create more understanding between you and your parents. Let them know how you feel, what is bothering you, and why so that open and honest dialogue can begin.

### Activity 7: Conflict Resolution Strategies

Conflict means two or more people disagree about a specific behavior or situation. Resolving the conflict means that all parties involved feel like justice has occurred. The following exercise is a guide to amicably resolving conflicts:

- First, you must define the problem accurately. Give each person in the conflict an opportunity to explain their issue. This discussion should continue until everyone is on the same page about the description of the conflict.
- Resolving the conflict should be done in a neutral place where nobody has an advantage. It helps to have an unbiased mediator present as well.
- A solution must then be developed for all parties involved. This can be a compromise or even an agreement to part ways.

These three key considerations can be applied to a variety of conflicts as a tool to work through fights and maintain relationships.

# Setbacks in Life

Everything will not always go as planned, especially if you have big, ambitious goals. Dealing with failure and setbacks is the way to success. You cannot let a pothole disrupt your entire journey. You must fix the flat tire it caused and keep going. Setbacks are overcome with an unstoppable drive to continue.

### Activity 8: Become Resilient

Resilience is the ability to withstand hardship. The only way to develop resilience is by going through difficulties and persevering. To become more resilient, you need to do something challenging that you don't like every day. Doing that is practice for the times when you will experience hardships.

Write down a difficult task that you can perform daily. For example, you can write down exercising if you do not enjoy physical activity.

Set an hour a day to complete this task.

When this task becomes easier, increase the difficulty or find something else challenging.

### Activity 9: Rebuilding

There will be occasions in life when you royally mess up and have to start over. For example, you might want to start a small business, but your plan falls apart for various reasons. When you fail, go through this protocol to rebuild:

- Write down the details of your failure.
- Why did this failure happen?
- Could it have been worse?
- Could it have been better?
- Is there any way this could have been prevented?
- What changes can you make in your mindset and behavior to address this failure?
- How can you prevent this from occurring in the future?
- What steps will you take to remedy the situation and rebuild yourself back up?
- What changes can you make today to work toward rebuilding?

# Stress Management

Stress can be described as the mental strain felt when a person excessively worries about a task, person, or situation. Your family, social, and school life can be overwhelming at times. The pressure from all the voices pulling you in different directions and the need to succeed can cause constant stress. Finding ways to cope with your stress is key to developing the character needed to tackle all challenges.

The pressure from all the voices pulling you in different directions and the need to succeed can cause constant stress.

## Activity 10: Stress Management Techniques

Stress can increase when you feel like a task is unmanageable. Breaking big activities into smaller, manageable chunks is a great way to manage that.

- Write down the anxiety-inducing task.

- Break it down into weekly goals.

- Write down what you can do daily to achieve your weekly goals.

- Set time apart from your schedule for the activities you must complete daily.

- By managing your time well, you can significantly reduce stress and can be more productive.

Adversity is part of life. Running from struggles is an impossible task that will have the negative side effect of hindering your progress. Finding ways to deal with conflict, stress, and negative emotions all stem from being aware of yourself, your environment, and society. Embracing awareness, communicating well, planning, and executing are the pillars of building the resilience needed to leap over all hurdles and smash through the walls that hold you back.

# Section 6: Financial Wisdom

In the journey of life, one of the most essential skills teens must master is the art of managing finances. Money may not be the key to happiness, but it undoubtedly plays a pivotal role in shaping the course of life. As you stand at the threshold of a world filled with financial choices and responsibilities, the decisions made now, no matter how small they may seem, can profoundly impact your future. In this section, you will delve into the realm of financial wisdom, equipping you with the knowledge and skills necessary to navigate the complex world of money with confidence and prudence.

Money may not be the key to happiness, but it undoubtedly plays a pivotal role in shaping the course of life.
*https://unsplash.com/photos/green-plant-in-clear-glass-vase-ZVprbBmT8QA*

### The Power of Financial Literacy

Understanding money empowers you to make informed decisions about your finances, whether it's budgeting for a new video game, saving up for college, or even starting your own business someday.

Financial literacy means knowing how to manage your money wisely, a skill that will serve you throughout your life. It helps you avoid debt, plan for your goals, and achieve financial security.

### Why Financial Literacy Matters

Financial literacy isn't just about math; it's about shaping your future. It gives you the tools to make choices that align with your goals and values. It's the key to financial independence, allowing you to create the life you want. So, whether you dream of traveling the world, starting a nonprofit, or simply living comfortably, understanding money is your first step toward making those dreams a reality.

# Basics of Budgeting

Money management might not sound thrilling, but it's the secret to realizing your financial dreams. It all starts with budgeting. This section will break down the basics of budgeting and guide you on creating a personal budget that sets you on the path to financial success.

### Understanding Budgeting

Think of a budget as your financial plan. It's a roadmap that tells your money where to go. Budgeting helps you:

1. **Track Your Income:** Know how much money you have coming in, whether it's from allowances, part-time jobs, or gifts.

2. **Plan Your Expenses:** Decide where your money should go, like saving for a new gaming console, covering school expenses, or setting aside some cash for a rainy day.

3. **Stay on Course:** Budgeting helps you avoid overspending and accumulating debt.

# Creating Your Personal Budget

Now, to get practical, here's how to create your personal budget:

- **List Your Income:** Start by regularly writing down all the money you receive. This includes allowances, earnings from odd jobs, or any other sources of income.

- **Track Your Expenses:** Make a list of your expenses. Start with the essentials like school supplies, transportation, and savings for long-term goals. Then, add your discretionary spending, like entertainment, snacks, and non-essential purchases.

- **Set Goals:** What do you want to achieve with your money? Maybe it's saving up for a new gaming console, contributing to a charity you care about, or building an emergency fund. Your goals will guide your budget.

- **Income vs. Expenses:** Compare your total income to your total expenses. Ideally, you want your income to exceed your expenses, leaving room for savings and fun spending. If expenses are higher, it's time to make adjustments.

- **Allocate Your Money:** Distribute your income to different categories based on your priorities. Make sure you allocate funds for savings and emergencies before discretionary spending.

- **Track and Adjust:** Your budget isn't set in stone. Track your spending regularly and adjust your budget as needed. If you overspend in one category, adjust by spending less in another.

- **Save and Invest:** Watch your savings grow as you stick to your budget. Consider putting some of your savings into a savings account or exploring beginner investment options to make your money work for you. You can discuss your savings goals with your parents or caregivers so they can help you open a savings account.

Budgeting might seem daunting at first, but with practice, it becomes a valuable skill that sets you up for financial success. Remember, it's not about restricting yourself but about ensuring your money serves your goals and dreams. So, start budgeting today and watch your financial future unfold.

# Legit Ways to Earn

- **Part-Time Jobs:** You can find part-time employment opportunities in your local community. Jobs like working at a grocery store, a restaurant, or a retail shop provide valuable work experience and teach responsibility.

- **Babysitting or Pet Sitting:** Caring for children or pets in the neighborhood can be a rewarding and flexible way to earn money. It requires responsibility and the ability to manage tasks efficiently.

- **Lawn Care and Yard Work:** Offering lawn mowing, leaf raking, or gardening services to neighbors is an excellent way to earn money while getting some fresh air and exercise.

- **Tutoring:** If you're good at a particular subject, you can offer tutoring services to younger students who need help with their studies. Tutoring not only earns money but also reinforces the value of education.

- **Freelancing and Gig Work:** You can explore online platforms to offer graphic design, content writing, or social media management services. These platforms allow you to leverage your skills and creativity.

- **Arts and Crafts:** If you have artistic talents or crafting skills, you can create and sell artwork, jewelry, or other handmade items online or at local craft fairs.

- **Car Washing and Detailing:** Offering car washing and detailing services to family and friends can be a profitable venture that teaches you attention to detail and customer service.

- **Online Surveys and Market Research:** Some websites offer paid surveys and market research opportunities for teens to earn money by providing opinions on various products and services.

- **Babysitting Apps:** There are mobile apps that connect babysitters with parents in need of childcare services. You can register on these apps and find babysitting opportunities in your area.

- **Online Content Creation:** If you have a passion for video creation or blogging, you can start your own YouTube channel, blog, or social media account. Once you gain a following, you can earn money through advertising and sponsorships.

- **Local Events and Festivals:** You can explore opportunities to work at local events, such as festivals, concerts, or sports games, as ticket takers, concession stand workers, or event assistants.

- **Virtual Assistance:** Offering virtual assistance services like email management, appointment scheduling, or data entry can be a remote way to earn money and develop organizational skills.

There are numerous free-to-access and paid online resources that you can use to learn these skills. You can ask your parents, caregivers, or teachers to guide you in finding the right learning platform.

These opportunities will teach you the importance of responsibility, time management, and the value of earning money through hard work. By understanding that hard work pays off, you can develop a strong work ethic that will serve you well throughout your life.

# Understanding Finances

### Short-Term vs. Long-Term Savings

Understanding the difference between short-term and long-term savings is key to financial success. Short-term savings are like your quick-access funds, usually meant for goals you want to achieve within the next year or so. It could be saving up for a new gaming console, a school trip, or even a special gift. Long-term savings, on the other hand, are your secret weapon for the future.

Think of it as the nest egg you're building for goals that are several years down the road, like college tuition, buying a car, or even your dream home.

### Setting SMART Financial Goals

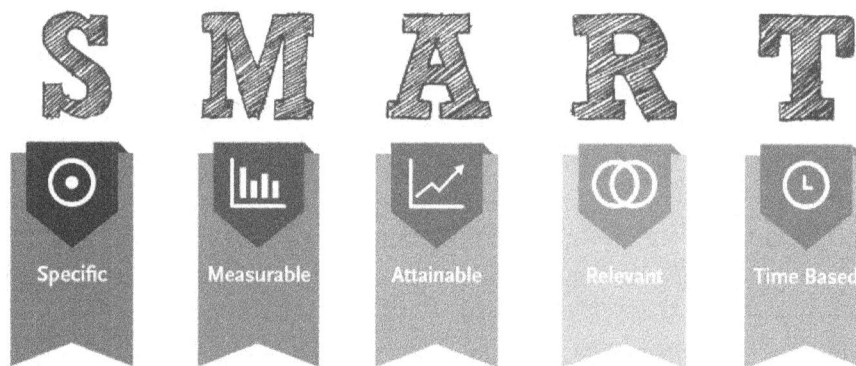

**Your goal should matter to you and align with your values.**
*Dungdm93, CC BY-SA 4.0 <https://creativecommons.org/licenses/by-sa/4.0>, via Wikimedia Commons:*
*https://commons.wikimedia.org/wiki/File:SMART-goals.png*

Use the SMART criteria to make your goals Specific, Measurable, Achievable, Relevant, and Time-bound:

- **Specific:** Define exactly what you want. Instead of "I want to save money," say, "I want to save $500 for a new gaming console by the end of the year."

- **Measurable:** Make your goal quantifiable so you can track your progress. In the previous example, you can easily measure how close you are to $500.

- **Achievable:** Make sure your goal is realistic and attainable based on your current income and expenses. Saving $500 may be more achievable than saving $5,000 in the same time frame.

- **Relevant:** Your goal should matter to you and align with your values. If gaming is your passion, saving for a console is relevant. Likewise, if you love traveling, saving for a trip you always wanted to make is relevant.

- **Time-bound:** Set a clear deadline. When do you want to achieve this goal? It can be next week, by the end of the month, or within three months.

# Introducing Banking and Financial Accounts

Banking and financial accounts are your tools for keeping your money safe, organized, and working for you. Here are the basics:

- **Savings Account:** Think of a savings account as your treasure chest. It's a safe place to keep your money while earning some interest. You'll use this for your short-term and emergency savings goals. Several types of savings accounts have varying interest rates, associated fees, and miscellaneous charges.

- **Checking Account:** This is basically your daily wallet. You use it for everyday expenses, like buying lunch or snacks. It's easy to access and often comes with a debit card for payments.

- **ATM:** Automated Teller Machines, or ATMs, are like cash vending machines. You can withdraw money, check your balance, and even deposit cash or checks at some ATMs.

- **Online and Mobile Banking:** Many banks offer online and mobile banking apps. These let you check your accounts, transfer money, and pay bills from your phone or computer. These apps and online banking facilities are convenient but must be used responsibly, as small mistakes or the inability to keep your credentials safe can be dangerous.

- **Interest:** Some accounts, like savings accounts, earn interest. It's like a bonus the bank gives you for keeping your money with them. The more you save, the more interest you earn.

- **Fees:** Be aware of any fees associated with your accounts. Some accounts charge fees if you don't maintain a certain balance or exceed a certain number of transactions.

By understanding the difference between short-term and long-term savings, setting SMART financial goals, and getting acquainted with banking and financial accounts, you're well on your way to mastering your money and achieving your financial dreams. Remember, money is a tool you control, and with knowledge and planning, you can make it work.

# Practicing Responsible Spending

Responsible spending is all about making thoughtful choices with your money to ensure it aligns with your goals and values. Here are some strategies to help you make informed spending decisions:

### Create a Budget

Develop a budget that outlines your income, expenses, and savings goals. You can try the 50/30/20 rule when budgeting. Allocate half of the budget towards your needs, around 30% to your wants, and the rest as savings for a rainy day. Lastly, don't forget to track where your money goes to prevent overspending.

### Differentiate Wants vs. Needs

Before making a purchase, ask yourself if it's something you truly need or if it's more of a want. Prioritize needs over wants to ensure essential expenses are covered first.

### Set Spending Limits

Establish spending limits for discretionary categories like entertainment, dining out, or shopping. Stick to these limits to avoid impulsive purchases.

### Shop with a List

Whether you're grocery shopping or buying clothes, having a list helps you stay focused and reduces the chances of buying unnecessary items.

### Delay Gratification

When tempted to make an impulse purchase, give yourself time to think it over. You can recall the wants vs. needs criteria mentioned earlier or review your budget to know how much extra money you must spend on that item. Delaying gratification often leads to more thoughtful spending decisions.

### Comparison Shopping

Before buying a big-ticket item, research and compare prices from different sellers to ensure you get the best value. If you're struggling with price comparisons, find apps that provide a price comparison specific to your location to snag deals on the items you want to buy.

### Avoid Credit Card Debt

Credit cards can be convenient, but avoid carrying a balance and accruing interest charges. Pay your credit card bill in full each month to maintain financial discipline. On-time payments will also improve your credit score, which most banks and financial institutions check when giving credit.

### Track Your Spending

Use apps or spreadsheets to monitor your spending habits. This helps you identify areas where you can cut back and save more.

### Aligning Financial Choices with Personal Values

Your financial choices should reflect your personal values and what matters most to you. Here's how to ensure your spending aligns with your values:

- Take time to reflect on your core values. What are the things that matter most to you in life? It could be family, education, health, travel, or charitable giving.
- Once you've identified your values, prioritize them. Determine which values are most important to you and should guide your financial decisions.
- Allocate a portion of your budget to support your values. For example, if education is a top priority, allocate funds for tuition, books, and educational resources.
- As your income grows, resist the temptation to increase your spending on non-essential items. Instead, channel the extra income toward your values-based goals.
- Periodically review your financial goals and spending habits. Make adjustments as needed to ensure your money aligns with your evolving values.
- If philanthropy or helping others is valuable, consider allocating a portion of your budget to charitable donations or volunteering your time to causes you care about.

By incorporating these strategies, you'll make responsible spending decisions and ensure that your money serves as a tool to support and amplify your values, ultimately leading to a more fulfilling and purpose-driven financial journey.

# Tackling Financial Emergencies

Handling unexpected financial emergencies can be challenging, but you can navigate these situations effectively with careful planning. Here's a step-by-step guide to help you prepare for and handle unexpected financial emergencies:

### Build an Emergency Fund

Before emergencies strike, establish an emergency fund. Your goal should be to have enough savings to cover around 6 months of expenses and keep these in a savings account. Start small if needed and gradually increase your savings over time. The key here is consistency. Establishing an emergency fund may take some time, but once achieved, it will provide you with financial stability in an emergency.

### Assess the Emergency

Determine the nature and scope of the emergency. Is it a medical expense, car repair, job loss, or other unforeseen events? Evaluate the urgency and impact of the situation to prioritize your response.

### Stay Calm

Take a deep breath and maintain a calm mindset. Panic can cloud your judgment. Gather information about the emergency, such as costs, deadlines, and available resources.

### Create a Financial Action Plan

Estimate the immediate financial needs associated with the emergency. This includes any bills, medical expenses, or repairs. Identify non-essential expenses that can be temporarily cut or reduced to redirect funds toward the emergency if possible.

### Use Your Emergency Fund

If you have an emergency fund, use it to cover immediate expenses. Transfer funds from your savings account to your checking account as needed. Be judicious in your spending, focusing on essential costs.

### Avoid High-Interest Debt

If you don't have an emergency fund, try to avoid turning to high-interest debt like credit cards. Interest can compound quickly and exacerbate your financial situation.

### Seek Additional Income

Consider taking on temporary work, gig jobs, or selling unused possessions to generate extra income. Contact friends and family for potential opportunities or support.

### Create a Long-Term Recovery Plan

Once the immediate emergency is under control, develop a plan to rebuild your finances and replenish it. Adjust your budget to accommodate both regular expenses and savings for future emergencies.

### Learn from the Experience

Reflect on the emergency and your response. Consider what could have been done differently to be better prepared in the future. Use the experience as motivation to strengthen your financial resilience and increase your emergency fund over time.

### Stay Committed

Continue to prioritize saving and building your emergency fund to be better equipped to handle future unexpected financial challenges.

Remember that unexpected emergencies are a part of life, and while they can be stressful, having a well-thought-out plan in place can help you navigate them with greater confidence and resilience.

# Section 7: Managing the House on Your Own

You must already know that your responsibilities increase as you get older. The more freedom you gain, the more consequences are on your shoulders. You are getting closer to one of the biggest tests of independence: living independently. That, obviously, comes with knowing how to manage your household. Stepping into this role blindly will cause unnecessary hiccups, but if you start to prepare now, you will be in a better position to run a home smoothly.

The more freedom you gain, the more consequences are on your shoulders.
https://unsplash.com/photos/people-sitting-on-chair-with-brown-wooden-table-mlVbMbxfWI4

Taking on some of the household work in your home can facilitate better relationships with the people you live with. You may already have chores that your parents or caregivers instruct you to perform. However, ask yourself if you did anything without being told to. Your surroundings reflect you, so managing where you live creates a space for self-expression. In a high-class restaurant kitchen, every station must be expertly prepped before one grain of rice is cooked, and all the utensils must be properly organized. Each staff member knows their job, so the operation can run like a machine. Similarly, if you manage your house well, you can be more productive and able to segment your time to follow your passions.

# Household Chores

Researchers at Princeton University found that a cluttered environment can make it difficult to focus on tasks and is often linked to tension and irritability (Gordon, 2023). Therefore, staying on top of your chores is a way to maintain positivity and make room for creativity to thrive. There are many things in the world that you cannot control. Getting lost in this sense of hopelessness can be prevented by taking hold of what you have power over. Suppose you want to chase the dream of significantly impacting and shifting society. In that case, you must grow outward from a central point. So, before you can change the world, you must be able to look after where you live. How can people trust you in higher positions of authority when you do not take direct responsibility for the small things within your reach?

### Activity 1: Collaborating on Chores

Unless you live alone, which is seldom the case for most people, you have to cooperate with other individuals in your home, whether they are family, friends, or roommates. The flames of conflict can easily be stoked when it is unclear what the responsibilities of each person in the household are.

Separating tasks can lessen the workload for the members of the household. When people are overwhelmed with chores, it's much easier to maintain a peaceful environment. If you get home before your parents, you can take on some of the responsibility at home.

Speak to your parents, siblings, or anyone else you live with about what each person is expected to do when it comes to chores.

Write down each individual's daily and weekly tasks in detail. Create a chart uniquely catered to anything home-related. On the chart, add each person's name, their daily chores, and space to tick off each one.

This chart will allow you to hold yourself and others accountable for what they are expected to do daily.

### Activity 2: Setting Time for Chores

Now that you have created a chore chart, calculate how long it will take you to do each task. Dedicate the same time every day for chores. That will help you build a strong routine and positive habits. You will also be able to spend the rest of your time on any other responsibilities you have.

# Cooking, Meal Planning, and Grocery Shopping

Nutrition is the foundation of health. Meal planning, cooking, and grocery shopping are underrated skills that can impact all the other spheres of your life. Both your physical and mental health are greatly impacted by the food that you eat. Moreover, a large chunk of your budget will go to your groceries, so buying the right food also has a financial aspect to it. Meal planning, shopping, and cooking all revolve around the cost of your food, its nutritional quality, and time management.

### Activity 3: Budgeting and Meal Planning

The next time your parents go grocery shopping, go with them and keep the receipt. Take some time to review all the items on it and add up the cost of the things you use. With the allowance you get or the money from your job, determine how much you can contribute if you have one. Even if you can't contribute anything, you will at least get a rough idea of the cost of being independent.

Meal planning is central to nutrition. Your goal is to plan your meals and make sure that they contain all the calories you need and the essential nutrients: vitamins, minerals, carbohydrates, proteins, and fats.

A balanced diet gives you the energy to complete all the tasks you need to tackle for the day. Food is the body's fuel, so high-quality meals will keep your mind sharp and your body strong. It is surprising how much more productive you can be if you eat well. Track what you eat for the week. There are useful apps available online that can help you track calories and nutrition. Google the amount of calories you should eat in a day and the amount of each essential nutrient you need per day.

- Does your diet meet or exceed the calorie requirements?
- Do you get enough of each nutrient?

What changes can you make to your most common meals to make them healthier? Remember, doing enough research and consulting medical professionals when creating meal plans is crucial.

### Activity 4: Cooking

Knowing how to cook is an essential life skill for every adult. Not only can you better curate the quality of your food when you cook at home, but you can also save a lot of money by not always having to buy takeout.

Challenge yourself each week. Learning how to cook is now simpler than ever because any recipe is a YouTube search away. Whether you know how to cook already or not, this challenge can help you increase the number of meals you can make. Set one day aside per week to cook a new recipe. Set a budget, and keep the ingredients within that range.

Cooking a new recipe every week will keep your mind engaged, increase the number of meals you can make, and teach you how to budget better.

# Home Maintenance and Basic Repairs

Your teen years are the transitory phase into adulthood. While you are still young, you should use the opportunity to learn about home maintenance as much as possible to be fully equipped when you move into your own place one day. If you maintain your home regularly, you reduce the risk of having a budget-breaking catastrophe. Constantly working on small fixes in your home will help you dodge the avalanches that pile up with neglect.

### Activity 5: Home Maintenance Checklist

Daily home maintenance includes regular chores like cleaning, laundry, and yard work. However, some more substantial tasks need your consideration to keep a house in order. Slowly, over time, nature will have its impact on a home. Nothing lasts forever, so key parts of a house need to be regularly checked, repaired, or replaced. You can create a list of all the maintenance a home needs to ensure you do not miss anything or overlook the details of what is needed for a fully functional house.

Go through the following checklist and see what needs to be done.

- Are the gutters clean?
- Are there any chipped or peeling walls around the property?
- Do the fences or walls need repairing?
- Have any light bulbs gone out?
- Is the extractor fan above the stove clean and grime-free?
- Are all your pipes and faucets functional and not leaking?
- Is there any mold in your home?
- Are the electrical components fully functional?
- Are there any pests or infestations that need to be addressed?
- Do all the cupboard doors have handles, and are the hinges functional?
- Is your roof leak-free?

### Activity 6: Weekend Repair Challenge

Ask your parents or caregivers if any issues in your home need addressing. This could be some lights that need to be changed, gutters that must be cleaned, or some sections of your home that must be painted. Commit to taking care of one of the more manageable issues required in your home over a weekend. If the task is too overwhelming, you can recruit the help of some friends or family members. Dedicating a weekend to home maintenance is a sign of responsibility. This could lead to your parents or guardians trusting you more and allowing you to act with a higher level of autonomy.

# Safety and Emergency Preparation

To prevent getting caught in life-threatening confusion when things go wrong, you must be aware of safety and be prepared for all common emergencies. Fires and injuries occur relatively regularly, so part of managing a household means consciousness of danger. Just like there are fire and emergency drills at your school, these plans should also be implemented at your home. People feel comfortable in their houses, so it is easy to overlook pressing risks. For your peace of mind and the safety of yourself as well as those around you, being prepared is crucial.

### Activity 7: Emergency Exits and Safety Protocols

Every home is unique, so making a protocol that works for all homes is difficult. However, there are some basic tips to consider. Create a fire exit framework for you and your family to follow. Use the following tips to draft the safest plan possible.

- Create two or more exits out of every room. You can use ladders or steps to do this.
- Find ways to navigate your home while being low to the ground.
- Establish a meeting point at a safe distance from your home in case of fire.
- Practice exit drills with your family.
- Install smoke alarms if possible.
- Make sure everyone in your home is aware of the safety protocols.

## Activity 8: First Aid Kit and Injury Preparedness

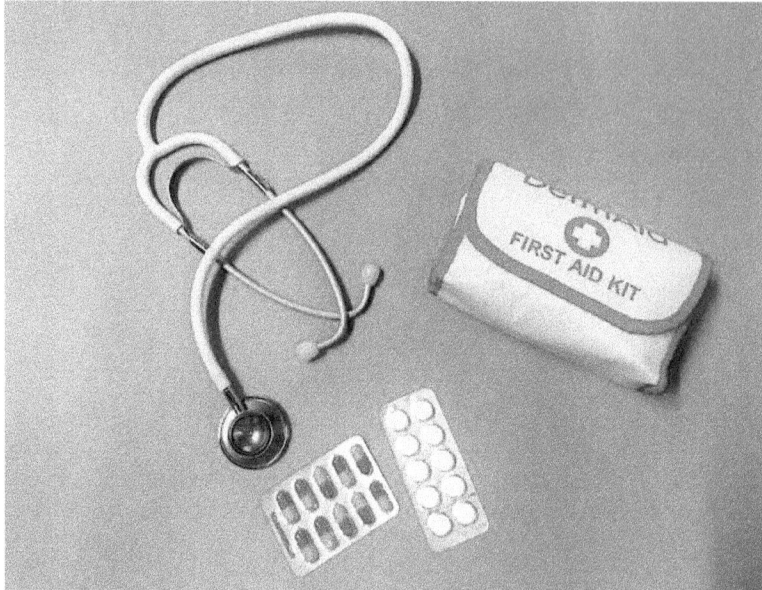

No one plans on getting hurt, but you have to be prepared in case it happens.
*https://unsplash.com/photos/a-bag-of-pills-a-stethoscope-and-a-first-aid-kit-ZvxNWi3JCto*

No one plans on getting hurt. One moment, you are having a great time, and the next second, someone has a huge gash on their arm. If you are an active or adventurous person, you may have some experience with injuries. When you were a little child, your parents or guardians ensured they mended your wounds when you got injured. Most households with young children will have an easily accessible first aid kit in the medicine cabinet. Most pharmacies sell full-stocked first aid kits, but there may come moments when you will have to restock them. Go through the list and see what you have at home. Ask your parents or use your pocket money to replace any missing items.

- Compress dressings
- Adhesive bandages
- Band-Aids
- Adhesive cloth tape
- Antibiotic ointment
- Antiseptic wipes
- Aspirin
- Emergency blanket
- Instant cold compress
- Gauze
- Tweezers
- Scissors
- Burn ointment
- First aid instruction manual
- Rehydration packets

# Time Management Strategies

As you age, you become increasingly conscious of how limited time is. If you can think back to when you were about five years old and someone told you to wait five minutes, how long did it feel? Compare that to now when five minutes flies by in the snap of a finger. Growing up means taking more on your plate. As the game of juggling responsibilities becomes harder, time management skills can be lifesaving. When your time is managed correctly, you have the benefit of being productive and avoiding stress, anxiety, and depression.

Time management can not be learned overnight. It takes some practice and getting used to discipline yourself enough to stick to a schedule. Getting the most out of your day makes every minute precious, so there is no time to waste. The difference between people who reach the highest levels of success and those who are mediocre is not skill or intelligence. *It is the time they are willing to put into what they love.* Reaching what you want for yourself requires you to be committed. However, you also need some downtime to relax and prevent burnout, so work recreational time into your schedule as well.

## Activity 9: Limiting Screen Time

The smartphone is the biggest thief of time and attention in the modern age. Social media and technology companies specifically design software that appeals to the most primal parts of the human mind. To manage your time efficiently, you need to significantly reduce your time staring at a screen.

There are some apps available online that can help you with regulating your screen time.

Select a two-hour segment in the day where you have to put away your phone and focus on a task that improves your mental or physical health. Practice this daily and notice how focused you can be when you don't allow your phone to distract you.

## Activity 10: Daily Schedule and Prioritizing

You probably have a lot that you want to achieve daily, weekly, monthly, and even yearly. You have commitments to school, your family, and friends, as well as any hobbies or extra-mural activities you participate in. Finding a balance between all these things requires you to prioritize. To effectively set your priorities, you must understand what your goals and visions for yourself are.

Right now, you may be in a phase in your life where you want to do it all. People have limited time, so it is impossible to do everything you want. Some of your desires will need to take a back seat because there are more important things. Analyzing what you cannot live without and what gives you meaning will determine what you spend most of your time on. Therefore, you must be able to set goals that can act as guiding signs to keep you going in the right way. Your goals should cover your social, financial, and school life.

- Write down one short-term goal to achieve in the next month, one medium-term in the next six months, and a long-term one to complete in a year or two.
- Write down a list of ten social, financial, familial, and educational tasks you have to complete within the next few months.
- According to the goals you have written for yourself, rank these tasks starting from most to least important. You can now measure where you should spend most of your attention.
- Keeping in mind your priorities and goals, compile a daily schedule. Plan out every hour of your day. Include time to rest, sleep, eat, do chores and homework, exercise, and any other

tasks you need to complete. Take your time creating your schedule and think deeply about it. Once it is complete, stick it on a wall or door where it is always visible. A schedule is useless if you do not follow it.

Running a successful household requires you to have clear goals, plan effectively, and manage your time well. As your responsibilities increase and you become more independent, there are many new considerations that you will need to make. You do not want to be in a position of having your own space – and feeling clueless! Now is the time to begin practicing maintaining a home. Finding time to spend with friends and family while focusing on schoolwork and hobbies can be difficult. You must take a measured approach to home management because the outcomes of handling your home life well will spill into all the other aspects of your life. The formula for managing yourself and your home well is visualizing, planning, executing, and then evaluating. By following these steps, you can craft a life you can take pride in while fulfilling your desires. Your home is the base from which you go on to conquer the world.

# Section 8: Survival Mindset and Skills

Survival skills can make you self-reliant and foster resilience, equipping you to navigate challenges and situations with competence and courage. Whether on the road, at home, in the wilderness, at home, or on the road, these invaluable skills can make all the difference. This chapter encompasses essential techniques and survival skills like constructing shelters, salvaging edible foods from the surroundings, starting a fire without matches, and purifying water for safe consumption. You'll also learn first aid skills to manage medical emergencies, injuries, calling for help, and much more. Survival skills are not just about overcoming extreme situations. They are tools for life. They foster resourcefulness, problem-solving, adaptability, and a deeper connection to the world around you.

Survival skills can make you self-reliant and foster resilience, equipping you to navigate challenges and situations with competence and courage.

https://unsplash.com/photos/man-walking-beside-graffiti-wall-0hQATQI7F7Q

# Basic First Aid and Wound Care

Unexpected accidents can lead to injuries, which can be managed when you know primary wound care and first aid. These skills can make a significant difference when it comes to preventing infections, minimizing pain, and even promoting healing. Here's an overview of essential first aid and wound care principles:

### Assess the Situation

Before rushing in to help, take a moment to assess the situation. Make sure it's safe for you and the injured person (if any). Look for potential hazards like traffic, fire, unstable structures, and barriers.

### Call for Help

Immediately call your local emergency number if the injury is severe, there is heavy bleeding, chest pain, spinal injury, loss of consciousness, severe burns, or difficulty breathing.

### Protect Yourself

If you have disposable gloves in your first aid kit, wear them to protect both yourself and the injured person. If gloves are unavailable, use a clean cloth or other barrier to minimize direct contact. Approach them calmly and confidently. Reassure them that you are there to help. Your presence and demeanor can reduce anxiety.

### Stop Severe Bleeding

Make sure that you put enough pressure on the wounded area. It's important to use your hand, a sterile gauze, or a clean cloth when it comes to excessive bleeding. Maintain pressure until the bleeding stops or help arrives. If possible, elevate the injury to control bleeding further. These maneuvers limit the blood flow toward the wound and decrease blood loss until emergency treatment is initiated.

### Clean the Wound

If the wound has dirt or debris, gently clean it with lukewarm water or a mild soap solution. Use a gauze present in the first aid kit to pat the area dry.

### Apply an Antibiotic Ointment

You can apply a thin layer of antibiotic cream or ointment to minimize wound exposure and the risk of infection. Avoid applying the ointment excessively, as it can suppress the healing process. However, avoid antibiotic ointment application if the wound is too deep, as it's meant for topical use. Instead, clean the wound with saline water or Pyodine solution until help arrives.

### Cover the Wound

After applying the ointment, use sterile gauze or a clean cloth to cover the wound. Make sure it's large enough to extend beyond the wound's edges. Secure the dressing in place with medical tape or a bandage.

### Elevate and Immobilize

If there's an injury to an extremity (arm or leg), elevate it to reduce swelling. Immobilize the injured limb with a splint if you suspect a fracture or to help manage pain. Several makeshift supports for an injured arm or leg can be made by salvaging materials from the surroundings, but it will require prior training.

### Monitor for Shock

Cover the injured person with a warm cloth or blanket, as in most cases, the body temperature drops after a physical injury. After covering, check for signs of pale skin, rapid breathing, shock, or confusion. If shock is suspected, keep the person lying down with their legs slightly elevated.

### Provide Comfort

Offer pain relief if needed and, if appropriate, follow the recommended dosage for over-the-counter pain medications like ibuprofen or acetaminophen.

### Seek Medical Attention

Even seemingly minor wounds may require medical attention as there may be a need for stitches or wound debridement (wound cleaning) to reduce the infection risk and to improve healing. Commonly, puncture wounds, bites, or deep cuts often warrant professional medical evaluation.

### Record Information

Keep a record of the injury details, such as the time it occurred, the severity of the injury, whether first aid was administered, and any signs or changes you notice in the person's condition. This information may be valuable to healthcare professionals, improving the outcomes.

Basic first aid aims to stabilize the injured person's condition and provide initial care until professional medical help arrives or until they can seek medical attention. It's essential to stay calm and confident, prioritize safety, and continuously monitor the injured person's condition while providing care. Taking a first aid course and regularly refreshing your skills is highly recommended to ensure you are prepared to handle various emergencies effectively.

# Assembling Emergency Kits

Being prepared for emergencies means having the right supplies readily available.

### Home Emergency Kit

- **Water:** Keep at least one gallon of water per person daily for at least three days.
- **Non-Perishable Food:** Include a three-day supply of canned or packaged food items like energy bars, canned fruits, and peanut butter.
- **Manual Can Opener:** Ensure you have a manual can opener if you pack canned goods.
- **Battery-Powered or Hand-Crank Radio:** This is essential for receiving emergency information and weather updates.
- **Flashlights:** Include extra batteries for your flashlights.
- **First Aid Kit:** Assemble a basic first aid kit with bandages, antiseptic wipes, adhesive tape, pain relievers, scissors, and tweezers.
- **Multi-Tool or Swiss Army Knife:** A versatile tool that can be handy for various tasks.
- **Blankets:** Keep warm blankets or sleeping bags in your kit.
- **Extra Clothing:** Pack spare clothing and sturdy shoes.
- **Personal Hygiene Items:** Include items like soap, toothbrushes, toothpaste, and sanitary supplies.
- **Important Documents:** Make copies of essential documents like identification, insurance policies, and medical records.

- **Cash:** Have some cash in small denominations available in case ATMs are not accessible.
- **Medications:** Store a week's supply of any prescription medications.
- **Whistle:** A whistle can help you signal for help if needed.
- **Matches or Lighter:** Include waterproof matches or a waterproof lighter.
- **Local Maps:** Maps of your area can be helpful if you need to move around.
- **Emergency Contacts:** Create a list of emergency phone numbers and addresses.
- **Pet Supplies:** If you have pets, pack food, water, and essential supplies for them.
- **Tools and Supplies:** Basic tools, duct tape, and plastic sheets can come in handy.

## School Emergency Kit

- **Water and Snacks:** Include a small bottle of water and non-perishable snacks like granola bars.
- **Personal Items:** Pack a small pouch with personal hygiene items like tissues, hand sanitizer, and a mask.
- **Emergency Contact Information:** Include a card with emergency contact names and phone numbers.
- **Whistle:** Attach a whistle to the outside of the kit for easy access.
- **Flashlight:** A small, battery-powered flashlight can be useful.
- **Notebook and Pen:** Include a small notebook and pen for taking notes or leaving messages.

## Outdoor Adventure Kit

- **Navigation Tools:** Carry a map, compass, and a GPS device if possible.
- **Shelter:** Include a lightweight, compact emergency shelter like a space blanket or bivvy.
- **Fire-Starting Supplies:** Waterproof matches, a lighter, and fire starters are essential.
- **Water Filtration:** Carry a portable water filter or purification tablets.
- **First Aid Kit:** A compact wilderness first aid kit that contains essentials like bandages, antiseptic wipes, and a CPR face shield.
- **Multi-Tool:** A multi-tool or Swiss Army knife is versatile and handy.
- **Food:** Pack high-energy snacks like trail mix, energy bars, and jerky.
- **Extra Clothing:** Include layers, a rain jacket, and a hat to stay warm and dry.
- **Emergency Communication:** Carry a whistle, signaling mirror, and a personal locator beacon (PLB) if necessary.
- **Headlamp:** A headlamp with extra batteries is useful for hands-free lighting.

Having these kits ready can make a significant difference in staying safe during emergencies, whether you're at home, school, or outdoors. Always stay informed about potential risks and adapt your emergency kits accordingly.

# Creating an Action Plan

## Step 1: Identify Potential Emergencies

Make a list of the possible emergencies that can occur in your home, school, or outdoors. These may include natural disasters (e.g., earthquakes, hurricanes), accidents (e.g., fires, car accidents), medical emergencies, or personal safety concerns.

Make a list of the possible emergencies that can occur in your home, school, or outdoors.
*https://unsplash.com/photos/person-writing-bucket-list-on-book-RLw-UC03Gwc*

## Step 2: Develop an Emergency Contact List

Create a list of important emergency contacts, including:

- Local emergency services (police, fire, medical).
- Family members and close friends' phone numbers.
- Schools or workplaces' emergency contacts.
- Healthcare providers' contact information.

## Step 3: Establish Communication Plans

Determine how your family, school, or adventure group will communicate during an emergency. Make sure everyone knows how to reach each other, even if separated. Designate a meeting point where everyone should gather if it's safe to do so.

## Step 4: Prepare Emergency Kits

As previously discussed, assemble emergency kits for home, school, and outdoor adventures. Ensure they contain necessary supplies, food, water, and first aid items.

## Step 5: Educate and Train

Educate family members, friends, or adventure companions about the emergency plans, including escape routes and communication procedures. Regularly practice emergency drills to ensure everyone knows what to do in various situations.

### Step 6: Stay Informed

Stay informed about potential emergencies in your area. Monitor weather alerts and stay updated on local news. Sign up for emergency alerts and notifications from relevant authorities.

### Step 7: Reacting to Emergencies

In an emergency, staying calm is crucial. Panic can lead to poor decision-making. Always follow the plan:

- Implement the emergency action plan you've established.
- Evacuate if necessary, or take shelter as directed.
- Keep in touch with family or group members using your designated communication methods.
- If it's safe, assist others needing help, especially the elderly, children, or individuals with disabilities.

### Step 8: Seek Professional Advice

For specific types of emergencies, consider seeking guidance from professionals or organizations specializing in safety, such as certified wilderness guides or emergency preparedness experts.

# Outdoor Survival Skills

Spending time in the wilderness can be thrilling, but being well-prepared and prioritizing safety is crucial. Here are some essential outdoor survival skills and safety tips to keep in mind:

### Starting a Fire

- Collect dry leaves, grass, and small twigs to use as tinder.
- Arrange your fuel wood in a teepee, lean-to, or log cabin style.
- Carry waterproof matches, a lighter, or fire starter sticks in your kit.
- Keep your fire contained and away from flammable materials. Always have water or sand nearby to extinguish it.

Spending time in the wilderness can be thrilling, but being well-prepared and prioritizing safety is crucial.
https://www.pexels.com/photo/black-kettle-on-the-camp-fire-11217391/

### Purifying Water

- Boiling water for at least one minute is the most effective way to purify it.
- Carry a portable water filter or purification tablets in case you can't start a fire.
- Use a clean container or rain tarp to collect rainwater.

### Basic Hunting Techniques

- Understand hunting regulations and laws in your area.
- Know how to use hunting tools safely, such as bows, firearms, or snares.
- Follow ethical hunting practices, including proper shot placement and humane harvesting.

### Navigation

- Learn to read maps and use a compass for navigation.
- Carry a GPS device as a backup, especially in unfamiliar terrain.
- Stick to established trails whenever possible.

### Shelter Building

- Learn how to construct simple shelters like lean-tos or debris huts.
- Utilize materials from the environment, such as branches and leaves.

Some other outdoor survival skills to keep in mind include:

- Before heading out, inform someone you trust about your plans, including your destination, expected return time, and emergency contact information.
- Carry enough water and drink it regularly to avoid dehydration.
- Be aware of wildlife in the area. Keep a safe distance, store food securely, and know how to react in case of encounters.
- Keep an eye on weather forecasts and be prepared for changing conditions.
- Protect yourself from insects with repellent, clothing, and proper campsite selection.
- Assess the terrain and plan routes accordingly. Avoid cliffs, unstable slopes, or areas prone to avalanches.
- Follow Leave No Trace principles to minimize your impact on the environment.
- Always carry a first aid kit with bandages, antiseptics, pain relievers, and personal medications.

Maintaining a survival mindset is crucial when exploring the outdoors. It is crucial for making rational decisions. Conserve energy, food, and water to maximize your chances of survival. *Furthermore, always carry signaling devices like whistles, mirrors, or personal locator beacons (PLBs) to attract attention if needed.*

# Prioritizing Personal Safety

Self-defense and personal safety are essential skills for protecting yourself and avoiding dangerous situations. Here are some key rules and guidelines to follow:

### Be Aware of Your Surroundings

One of the most important aspects of personal safety is situational awareness. Pay attention to your environment, including who is around you, potential escape routes, and any unusual or suspicious activity.

### Trust Your Instincts

Trust your gut instinct if something doesn't feel right or makes you uncomfortable. It's often better to err on the side of caution.

### Avoid Risky Areas and Situations

Stay away from areas known for high crime rates or that feel unsafe. Avoid walking alone at night in poorly lit or deserted areas.

### Walk with Confidence

Walk with purpose and confidence. Predators are less likely to target individuals who appear strong and assertive.

### Use Technology Wisely

Be cautious when using headphones or looking at your phone while walking, especially in unfamiliar areas. These distractions can make you an easy target.

### Stay Connected

Let someone know your whereabouts and estimated return time when you're going out alone. Share your location using a tracking app if necessary.

### Carry Personal Safety Items

Consider carrying personal safety items like a whistle, personal alarm, or self-defense tools (e.g., pepper spray or personal alarms) where legal.

### Keep a Safe Distance

Maintain a comfortable personal space bubble, and be cautious of anyone who invades that space.

### Learn Basic Self-Defense

A self-defense class can boost your confidence and provide practical skills to defend yourself if necessary.

### Use Verbal Communication

If confronted, use strong, assertive verbal communication to set boundaries and discourage potential attackers.

### Escape Is the Priority

Your primary goal in dangerous situations should be to escape, not fight. Avoid physical confrontation at all times.

### Self-Defense Techniques

If physical self-defense is necessary, target an attacker's vulnerable areas (e.g., eyes, throat, groin) and aim to escape as quickly as possible.

### Practice Self-Control

While self-defense skills are valuable, using them responsibly and only in situations where your safety is at risk is essential.

### Be Prepared for Emergencies

Carry a basic first aid kit, know how to use it, and have an emergency plan in case you or someone you're with is injured.

### Don't Hesitate to Seek Help

If you feel threatened or have been the victim of a crime, don't hesitate to call 911 or your local emergency number. Your safety is paramount.

### Avoid Substance Abuse

Alcohol and drugs impair judgment and reaction times, making you more vulnerable.

### Travel Safely

When traveling, research the safety of your destination, avoid risky areas, and take precautions to protect your belongings.

# Vehicle Maintenance

Vehicle maintenance and knowing what to do in emergencies are essential skills every driver needs to learn. Here are instructions on basic vehicle maintenance and emergency procedures:

### Checking Oil

1. Park your vehicle on a level surface and turn off the engine.
2. Open the hood and locate the oil dipstick.
3. Pull out the dipstick, wipe it clean with a cloth or paper towel, and reinsert it.
4. Pull it out again and check the oil level. It should fall within the marked range. If it's low, add the recommended oil for your vehicle.
5. Make sure the oil cap is securely tightened, and close the hood.

### Changing a Flat Tire

Gather the required tools to change the flat tire.
https://pixabay.com/photos/wheel-breakdown-automobile-1017023/

1. Gather the required tools to change the flat tire. These tools include a spare tire, lug wrench, and a jack to lift the flat tire for replacement.

2. Most vehicles have these tools in the trunk, including a spare tire.

3. You'll see four nuts securing the tire to the wheel hub. In a crisscross fashion, loosen the nuts one by one.

4. Each vehicle has a lift point where you can place the car jack and lift the car to the desired height. If you don't know the exact spot, the car's manual will help.

5. Lift the vehicle using the jack to a height where the flat tire can't touch the ground.

6. Remove the already loose lug nuts using the wrench.

7. The flat tire can now freely come off. Replace the flat tire with the spare one and secure the flat tire in the vehicle's trunk.

8. Using your hands, screw the nuts to keep the spare tire in place and lower the vehicle.

9. Now, use the wrench to tighten the nuts in a crisscross pattern.

10. Remove the jack from under the vehicle and place the tools you used back in the trunk.

The first thing you must do after replacing the tire is to find a tire repair shop and get the flat tire checked for damage. If it's a regular puncture and the tire condition is great, it can be repaired, or you may need to replace the tire with a new one.

## Jump-Starting a Vehicle

1. To jump-start a vehicle, you'll need an already-running car with a fully charged battery.

2. Park both cars side-by-side and switch off the engines.

3. Grab the red jumper cable and attach it to the dead battery's positive terminal. The other end needs to be attached to the working car's positive terminal.

4. Attach one end of the black jumper cable to the working battery's negative terminal.

5. The other end of the black cable must be attached to the dead vehicle's metal surface.

6. Start the working car, put it in neutral gear, and let it run for a few minutes.

7. After a few minutes, try starting the car you want to jump-start. If all the steps are executed correctly, the car with the dead battery will jump-start. Remember to remove the jumper cables in reverse order.

8. Keep the vehicle running and seek the nearest battery mechanic to inspect the battery's health and to avoid running into situations like these again.

## Car Breakdown or Accident

- **Safety First:** If possible, move your vehicle to a safe location off the road. Turn on hazard lights.

- **Assess the Situation:** Check for injuries and provide assistance if necessary. Call 911 if there are injuries or significant damage.

- **Exchange Information:** If involved in an accident, exchange insurance and contact information with other parties.

- **Document the Scene:** Take photos of the accident or breakdown, including vehicle damage, license plates, and road conditions.

- **Notify Authorities:** Call the police or local authorities to report the incident if required.

- **Contact Roadside Assistance:** If your vehicle is inoperable, contact your roadside assistance provider for help with towing or repairs.
- **Stay Calm:** Keep a cool head, be polite, and avoid confrontations with others involved.

Remember that safety should always be the top priority in emergencies on the road. Following these procedures can help you stay safe and handle accidents and common car problems effectively.

# Section 9: Digital Literacy

The internet has become an extension of personal expression and identity. People use technology to socialize, find people with common interests, spread ideas, and do business. The ability to instantly communicate and reach people thousands of miles away and access geographical borders has reshaped media and social environments all around the world. Teenagers have been born into a world where the internet is integral to daily life. The online reality is fused with how young people form perceptions about the world. Therefore, being mindful of how the internet functions, its dangers, and how to use it to its full potential can impact the quality of your life.

The internet has become an extension of personal expression and identity.
*https://pixabay.com/photos/mobile-phone-smartphone-keyboard-1917737/*

As much as the internet is beneficial, it can be extremely detrimental. It's widely known that prolonged social media use can result in the development of depression. Moreover, there is a direct correlation between the rise in adolescent suicide and the popularization of social media. Correctly navigating the digital world is crucial for your mental and physical well-being. The aim of mindfully using the internet should be to maximize the benefits and minimize the dangers.

# Online Safety and Privacy

It may seem like the digital world is as anonymous as you want it to be, but there are always nefarious forces looking to take advantage of you. The internet can be a beacon of prosperity and enjoyment, but it is also full of scammers and criminals. You would not walk around in a shady, unknown neighborhood waving around cash recklessly. Similarly, you shouldn't be careless online. Technology is great, but your security should come first. When you get into a car, you put on a seatbelt. A car is a useful way to travel quickly and can open the way to freedom and independence. However, you must be aware of some dangers on the road.

There are endless horror stories online of people getting harassed. People's identities and pictures have been stolen and used to create accounts impersonating them. Unfortunately, individuals have been duped out of thousands of dollars by people selling fraudulent products or taking their money to deliver nothing. The ocean, which is the internet, allows you to cast your net out for connection and entertainment – *and it is also where criminals go to fish.* In addition to people deceptively contacting you to take advantage, viruses and spyware are designed to record and send your personal information to a third party.

Internet safety is based on a combination of being well-informed and taking precautions to avoid falling victim to the dark side of being online. You must take the necessary steps to protect your privacy while educating yourself on common techniques people use to gather the information they can use to exploit or manipulate you.

### Activity 1: Identifying Online Risks

Some of the primary risks found online are privacy breaches, deception, and groups looking to recruit impressionable people. To stay safe, there are a few things you can do:

- Install a VPN. VPN stands for "Virtual Private Network". This technology encrypts your online presence so that third parties do not make use of your data.
- Do not click on unknown links. Often, links that get sent to you through private messages contain malware.
- Avoid posting your location on social media. If you have strangers on any of your accounts, it could be dangerous to give away your location.
- Do not respond to anybody asking for private or sensitive information like your bank account or social security number.
- If it sounds too good to be true, it probably is. Many people have gotten scammed with promises of wealth or prizes.

Can you write down some risks to your financial, social, physical, and psychological safety online?

What measures can you put into place to prevent some of these risks?

### Activity 2: Protecting Your Personal Information

The beauty of many social media sites is that they facilitate how much of your life you want to share online and who you want to engage with. You can curate your social media accounts to protect your privacy. Giving out any personal information online is not advisable, even if it's people you trust, because *they* may have been hacked. Here are some questions you can ask yourself to protect your privacy.

- Who do I want to connect with on my page?
- What kind of people do I not want to associate with?
- How will the information I am sharing affect my future, and can it be used to harm me?
- How much do I want people online to know about my personal life?

# Cyberbullying Awareness

Cyberbullying is a modern occurrence where people are harassed, berated, and bullied using online platforms. These attacks can be random or targeted. Cyberbullying is especially dangerous now because of the always-online nature of modern life. In the past, someone may have been bullied at school, but they were able to escape when they got home. However, with cyberbullying, the harassment can be ceaseless and follow you wherever you go.

Cyberbullying is especially dangerous now because of the always-online nature of modern life.
https://www.pexels.com/photo/back-of-a-teenager-using-a-laptop-at-a-desk-6345305/

To curb cyberbullying, a two-pronged approach must be used. First, you should obviously not participate in bullying. Secondly, you must control your online environment. Think of all your online space, like your social media accounts, as your home. You wouldn't let someone dump trash onto your living room carpet.

Similarly, you cannot let people dump their garbage in the middle of your social media feed. The functions that tech companies provide let you completely control who you allow in. Social networks can quickly become toxic. *Take some regular breaks!*

### Activity 3: Dealing With Cyberbullying

Cyberbullying comes in different forms. It could be someone impersonating you and sending messages to people on your account, or people could be sending you harmful messages. There are physical, emotional, and mental consequences to cyberbullying. It could have detrimental psychological impacts like developing anxiety or depression. Targets of cyberbullying could also experience physical illness due to stress and anxiety.

- Do you feel like you have been cyberbullied?
- How did the bullying make you feel?
- Have you ever cyberbullied someone?

It is easy to fall into the habit of hurting others, especially if you have been hurt before. It is important to evaluate your behavior to make sure that you are not bullying others online. If you are being cyberbullied, here are some steps you can take:

- You can use the block button to get rid of anyone bothering you.
- Stay out of toxic online communities that are accustomed to being overly confrontational.
- Use your privacy settings to control who can DM you or who can comment on your posts.
- Report harassing messages or posts.
- Speak to people you trust, like parents, teachers, or friends, about what you are experiencing. Talking to people you can confide in about your problems can be therapeutic.

### Activity 4: Dangerous Online Communities

Ostracization and alienation can push many people to niche communities online. This is not always bad because it allows people to connect with like-minded people online and even make some friends along the way. However, destructive communities exist online. Many people have found their way into prejudiced and violent groups. Before joining an online community, ask these questions:

- Does this community align with the goals you've set for yourself?
- Are there bigoted or prejudiced views being promoted in this group?
- What kind of people usually interact in this group, and do you want to connect with them?
- How does the group treat members and people who are not part of the community?
- How do people in the community respond when you express views that are different from theirs?

Joining toxic communities online can lead to you developing and embracing inaccurate and dangerous views that have real-life consequences. Just like there are terrible people in real life, there are also misguided people online.

# Conscious Technology Use

Social media companies aim to keep you staring at the screen for as long as possible. When you spend extended periods online, these companies gather your data to sell it to others who make marketing decisions based on your online behavioral patterns. This technology has been designed to appeal to the parts of your brain that develop addiction. Understanding the addictive qualities of social media allows you to make decisions where you can control your technology use instead of it controlling you.

If you go to a shooting range, they will teach you exactly how to use a gun. They will go through all the safety protocols to prevent anybody from getting hurt because using a firearm in the wrong can seriously injure someone. The internet is the exact same way. Many people's lives have been derailed because of irresponsibly using the internet. Considering that the stakes can be exceedingly high when using these products that are developing exponentially each year, you must tread cautiously.

### Activity 5: Managing Screen Time

Have you ever been scrolling on TikTok, or whatever your preferred social media site is, and suddenly noticed that you have been doing that for hours? That lost time can be spent to better yourself or interact with your loved ones. You need to be mindful of how easily social media can consume your time.

- How much time do you spend online a day?
- How much of that time benefits you and is productive?

Take this challenge:

Set aside two hours of your free time per day, and don't use your phone at all. It will be difficult at first. Do whatever you want with this, whether it's school work, a hobby, or just sitting around to clear your head. Notice how you feel when you limit your time online.

### Activity 6: Setting Healthy Boundaries

Carrying your phone on you at all times can affect your life in a way that no other piece of technology can. Think about if you spent time with your best friend for days on end without taking your eyes off each other. Eventually, the relationship will become so toxic that you need to spend time apart, but you just don't know it. People do not apply the same limitations they have for friends and family to technology. Therefore, you must set some boundaries for yourself when using your devices.

- When have you used your phone at inappropriate times?
- Has your phone ever disrupted an active conversation?
- Does being without your phone negatively affect your mood?
- Write down when it is okay to use your phone and when it is not.
- Now, write down how many hours you currently spend online and how you can cut down on that time.

# Social Media Etiquette

One thing the last decade has taught humanity is that the internet never forgets. Whatever you post online can come back around to be used against you. You always need to conduct yourself appropriately online. In a way, you are creating a digital identity. Whenever you post something, you are contributing to how people perceive you. Thinking about what message and image you want to project online will guide the kinds of posts that you make.

Furthermore, how you engage with others will also affect how people see you. Do not allow the internet to drag you into posting things you will regret later or that can ruin your most treasured relationships. Practicing social media etiquette not only affects the way others perceive you but can also promote mental and emotional health online.

## Activity 7: Promoting Kindness

The internet can be the wild west at times. Much of the negative consequences of social media is that people allow themselves to be controlled by their darker impulses due to the safety provided by being behind a screen. By promoting kindness online, you can help shift the negative culture of social media spaces. To be kinder, there are a few adjustments you can make.

Ask these questions before messaging someone or posting something:

- Do you need to respond to this negative post or comment?
- How can you respond in a way that promotes positivity?
- How would I feel if someone said this to me?
- Why is this person responding negatively?
- Should you block and report this person to protect your mental health?

By promoting kindness online, you can help shift the negative culture of social media spaces.
https://unsplash.com/photos/person-reaching-black-heart-cutout-paper-XX2WTbLr3r8

## Activity 8: Curating Your Social Media Experience

Social media companies excel at allowing users to mold their experience. Think about some of the communities you have interacted with online. Some have encouraging and positive comment sections, while others have a hurtful and confrontational environment. This is all because of how the person who runs the account curated their social media experiences. Before posting online, ask yourself the following questions:

- What do you want my social media to feel like?
- Which kinds of comments will you allow?
- What type of language will you use to create a positive experience online?
- Which communities will you be a part of?
- How will what you post affect you in the future, and does it align with your vision for yourself?

# Critical Thinking and Media Literacy

The internet has allowed humanity to share more information than it ever could have imagined just a few decades ago. The people in charge of disseminating information have decentralized from big media houses to anybody who can post. In this flood of content, you need to develop critical thinking skills to be able to evaluate what is accurate and factual. Misinformation and conspiracy theories are so common that they can easily be taken at face value.

## Activity 9: Fake News and Critical Thinking

Both major news and alternative media are filled with biases. Everyone is trying to promote what they believe is right. Sometimes, people bend the truth to align with their agendas. This is why it is important to have critical thinking skills to get the most accurate picture of whatever story is presented before you. When watching a video or reading an article, the following questions will help you determine what is true:

Who is posting this story? A random blog is not as trustworthy as a major new website when it comes to accurate information. Scholarly websites that post peer-reviewed articles and studies are more trustworthy than both blogs and news sites. Furthermore, understanding who posts a story will tell you their biases. For example, Fox News will be more right-wing politically, while CNN will have a left-leaning bias.

The open-source nature of the internet allows anybody to post, which is great for free speech but terrible when it comes to facts. Everything you read should be taken with a grain of salt. Just because you saw something by a popular creator does not make it true. Doubt everything on the internet before you accept it as valid. Always assume that everything you see is fake until you can verify it.

When was this posted? Some information online is outdated, which, in certain cases, can make it false.

Why was it posted? You must be able to determine the reason a person posted something so that you will know what prejudices they might have.

## Activity 10: Fact Checking and Credibility

Never accept anything you read or watch online without doing further research. You cannot do a simple Google search to fact-check and know if something is credible. Search engines give you whatever you are looking for. Therefore, you must know how to research. As mentioned previously, scholarly sources are the best way to know if something is accurate. Google Scholar is a great online research tool.

- Go to Google and type in "Google Scholar."
- Search for a topic you are interested in.

All the sites that appear will have peer-reviewed research articles, which are some of the most trustworthy sources of information you can find on the internet.

With all the benefits that technology has provided, some dangers must be acknowledged. The melting pot of the online sphere creates a crazy world where all different kinds of people come together for different agendas and goals. You must use all the tools that social media companies provide and consistently inform yourself about scams. For your mental, emotional, and physical well-being to be maintained, your online behavior must be shaped to create a positive experience. Just like you wouldn't trust a stranger selling dreams on the side of the road, make sure you don't fall victim to lies and falsehoods online. The invention of social media has caused a rise in depression, anxiety, and suicide among teenagers, but if you take the time to be responsible online, you can avoid these negative consequences while maximizing the benefits of this technology.

# Thank You Message

Your commitment and dedication to finishing this book show that you are already on the path to becoming a confident, well-informed, and capable young man.

As you practice the lessons you've learned in the book, remember that knowledge is the first step toward personal growth and success. Each section holds valuable insights that will serve as your compass in navigating the turbulent waters of adolescence.

The sections in the book named Socialize Like a Pro and Digital Literacy equip you with skills to foster meaningful relationships and navigate the digital world responsibly. Financial Wisdom will enable you to handle money matters like a pro, ensuring your path toward financial security.

Managing the House on Your Own is more than just chores. It's about gaining independence and responsibility. Survival Mindset and Skills will instill courage and the right skills to handle challenges, while the Common Struggles section will provide you with impactful strategies to overcome obstacles.

Remember, this book isn't just about reading. It's about understanding and implementing what you've learned in your daily routine. Embrace the lessons shared to heart and use them enthusiastically. Every step you take toward self-improvement is a step toward your brighter future.

Your journey through adolescence may have its ups and downs, but with the wisdom gained from these pages, you have a powerful toolset to thrive. Embrace your potential, keep learning, and never forget that you have the power to shape your destiny.

If you enjoyed this book, I'd greatly appreciate a review on Amazon because it helps me to create more books that people want. It would mean a lot to hear from you.

**To leave a review:**

1. Open your camera app.
2. Point your mobile device at the QR code.
3. The review page will appear in your web browser.

*Thanks for your support!*

# Check out another book in the series

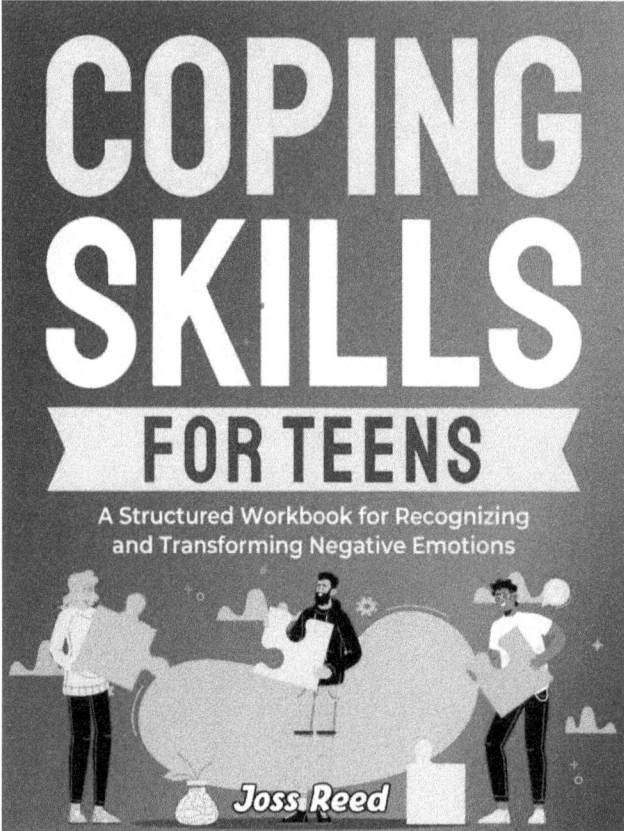

# References

(N.d.-a). Apa.org. https://www.apa.org/topics/bullying/prevent

(N.d.-a). Verywellfamily.com. https://www.verywellfamily.com/teaching-time-management-skills-to-teens-2608794

(N.d.-b). Apa.org. https://www.apa.org/topics/children/stress

(N.d.-b). Indeed.com. https://www.indeed.com/career-advice/career-development/conflict-resolution-strategies

(N.d.). Tomtrackout.com. https://www.tomtrackout.com/event/adulting-workshops-for-teens-personal-safety-and-self-defense/

10 critical thinking exercises to improve your mind. (2022). Indeed.com. https://uk.indeed.com/career-advice/career-development/critical-thinking-exercises

10 ways to cope with big changes. (n.d.). Psychology Today. https://www.psychologytoday.com/za/blog/here-there-and-everywhere/201701/10-ways-cope-big-changes

10 ways to engage teens in bushcraft & survival. (2023, May 17). Outdoortopia. https://www.outdoortopia.org/post/10-ways-to-engage-teens-in-bushcraft-survival

6 secrets to becoming an inspiring teen leader! (n.d.). We Think Twice. https://www.wethinktwice.acf.hhs.gov/6-secrets-becoming-inspiring-teen-leader

AACAP. (n.d.). Stress management and teens. Aacap.org. https://www.aacap.org/AACAP/Families_and_Youth/Facts_for_Families/FFF-Guide/Helping-Teenagers-With-Stress-066.aspx

Arlin Cuncic, M. A. (2010, May 10). 7 active listening techniques to practice in your daily conversations. Verywell Mind. https://www.verywellmind.com/what-is-active-listening-3024343

Azem, L., Al Alwani, R., Lucas, A., Alsaadi, B., Njihia, G., Bibi, B., Alzubaidi, M., & Househ, M. (2023). Social media use and depression in adolescents: A scoping review. Behavioral Sciences, 13(6), 475. https://doi.org/10.3390/bs13060475

Blanton, K. (n.d.). 5 financial goals for teens, young adults. Crr.bc.edu. https://crr.bc.edu/5-financial-goals-for-teens-young-adults/

Courtney E. Ackerman, M. A. (2017, December 18). 87 self-reflection questions for introspection [+exercises]. Positivepsychology.com. https://positivepsychology.com/introspection-self-reflection/

Crevin, M. (2020, July 14). 8 ways teens can improve their communication skills. Your Teen Magazine; Your Teen Media. https://yourteenmag.com/family-life/communication/ways-to-improve-communication

Cyberbullying: What is it and how to stop it. (n.d.). Unicef.org. https://www.unicef.org/end-violence/how-to-stop-cyberbullying

Damour, L. (2019, January 16). How to help tweens and teens manage social conflict. The New York Times. https://www.nytimes.com/2019/01/16/well/family/how-to-help-tweens-and-teens-manage-social-conflict.html

Definition of PEER PRESSURE. (n.d.). Merriam-webster.com. https://www.merriam-webster.com/dictionary/peer%20pressure

Emerson, M. S. (2021, August 30). 8 ways you can improve your communication skills. Professional Development | Harvard DCE. https://professional.dce.harvard.edu/blog/8-ways-you-can-improve-your-communication-skills/

Fletcher, J. (2022, May 13). What are the 6 essential nutrients? https://www.medicalnewstoday.com/articles/326132#:~:text=The%20six%20essential%20nutrients%20are,sources%20for%20proper%20body%20function.

Gongala, S. (2015, April 29). Sex education for teenagers – all you need to know. MomJunction. https://www.momjunction.com/articles/sex-education-for-teenagers_00352004/

Gordon, S. (2021, February 2). The connection between decluttering, cleaning, and mental health. Verywell Mind. https://www.verywellmind.com/how-mental-health-and-cleaning-are-connected-5097496

Grossman, A. L. (2021, March 8). Short-term financial goals for high school students (26 examples). Money Prodigy; Frugal Confessions, LLC. https://www.moneyprodigy.com/short-term-financial-goals-for-high-school-students/

Haelle, T. (2017, February 28). Online risks are everyday events for teens -- but they rarely tell their parents. Forbes. https://www.forbes.com/sites/tarahaelle/2017/02/28/online-risks-are-everyday-events-for-teens-but-they-rarely-tell-their-parents/?sh=1086aab33861

Helping kids cope with cliques. (n.d.). Kidshealth.org. https://kidshealth.org/en/parents/cliques.html

Hilliard, J. (2019, July 15). Social media addiction. Addiction Center. https://www.addictioncenter.com/drugs/social-media-addiction/

Home maintenance checklist. (n.d.). Leadhome Property Search. https://www.leadhome.co.za/blog/2021/07/06/5010/home-maintenance-checklist

Home wound care. (n.d.). Nationwidechildrens.org. https://www.nationwidechildrens.org/conditions/health-library/home-wound-care

How to be more empathetic. (n.d.). WebMD. https://www.webmd.com/balance/features/how-to-be-more-empathetic

Iannelli, V. (2007, August 9). How kids make and keep friends. Verywell Family. https://www.verywellfamily.com/making-and-keeping-friends-2633627

Internet and social media users in the world 2023. (n.d.). Statista. https://www.statista.com/statistics/617136/digital-population-worldwide/

Jain, P. (2022, October 14). Importance of financial literacy for teens. Times of India. https://timesofindia.indiatimes.com/blogs/voices/importance-of-financial-literacy-for-teens/

Kajal. (2019, October 12). Importance of social skills for students. |; The Asian School. https://www.theasianschool.net/blog/importance-of-social-skills-for-students/

Kevin. (2017, September 23). Online teen safety guide. Staysafe.org. https://staysafe.org/teens/

Koffman, M. (2022, April 12). Your child's social-emotional development. Braintrust. https://braintrusttutors.com/your-childs-social-emotional-development/

Langston, G. (2023a, January 11). A core values list will help your teen make better decisions. College Flight Plan. https://collegeflightplan.com/help-your-teen-determine-their-core-values-list/

Langston, G. (2023b, February 11). Strengths and weaknesses – Help your teen discover theirs. College Flight Plan. https://collegeflightplan.com/strengths-and-weaknesses-help-your-teen-discover-theirs/

Lenhart, A. (2015, August 6). Chapter 5: Conflict, friendships, and technology. Pew Research Center: Internet, Science & Tech. https://www.pewresearch.org/internet/2015/08/06/chapter-5-conflict-friendships-and-technology/

Lennarz, H. K., Hollenstein, T., Lichtwarck-Aschoff, A., Kuntsche, E., & Granic, I. (2019). Emotion regulation in action: Use, selection, and success of emotion regulation in adolescents' daily lives. International Journal of Behavioral Development, 43(1), 1–11. https://doi.org/10.1177/0165025418755540

Linehan, M. (n.d.). STOP skill. Dialectical Behavior Therapy (DBT) Tools; JW-Designs. https://dbt.tools/emotional_regulation/stop.php

Make a first aid kit. (n.d.). Redcross.org. https://www.redcross.org/get-help/how-to-prepare-for-emergencies/anatomy-of-a-first-aid-kit.html

Maruwada, M. (2021, September 25). 15 essential self care tips for teens and its importance. MomJunction. https://www.momjunction.com/articles/self-care-for-teenagers-students-tips_00772195/

Miranda. (2017, April 17). 6 activities to help teens to discover their passion. The Reluctant Cowgirl. https://thereluctantcowgirl.com/help-teens-discover-passion/

Money management for teenagers. (2023, March 16). Raising Children Network. https://raisingchildren.net.au/pre-teens/family-life/pocket-money/money-management-for-teens

Moore, C. (2019, February 19). Teaching Emotional Intelligence to teens and students. Positivepsychology.com. https://positivepsychology.com/teaching-emotional-intelligence/

Murawski, L. M. (n.d.). Critical thinking in the classroom...And beyond. Eric.ed.gov. https://files.eric.ed.gov/fulltext/EJ1143316.pdf

Nami, Y., Marsooli, H., & Ashouri, M. (2014). The Relationship between Creativity and Academic Achievement. Procedia – Social and Behavioral Sciences, 114, 36-39. https://doi.org/10.1016/j.sbspro.2013.12.652

Nonverbal communication and body language – Helpguide.org. (n.d.). https://www.helpguide.org/articles/relationships-communication/nonverbal-communication.htm

Parenting children through puberty and adolescence. (n.d.). Gov.au. https://www.betterhealth.vic.gov.au/health/healthyliving/Parenting-children-through-puberty

Paulus, N. (2022, February 16). Teens' guide to building a strong personal finance foundation. Moneygeek.com. https://www.moneygeek.com/financial-planning/personal-finance-for-teens/

Pontz, E. (2018, September 4). Strategies to handle peer pressure. Center for Parent and Teen Communication. https://parentandteen.com/handle-peer-pressure/

Practice your home fire escape plan. (n.d.). Ready.gov. https://www.ready.gov/home-fire-escape-plan

Puberty and teenagers. (n.d.). Reachout.com. https://parents.au.reachout.com/common-concerns/everyday-issues/puberty-and-teenagers

Riley Adams, C. P. A. (2023, May 12). Teenage money management & helpful financial planning apps. Young and the Invested. https://youngandtheinvested.com/teenage-money-management/

Rogers, C. J., & Hart, D. R. (2021). Home and the extended-self: Exploring associations between clutter and wellbeing. Journal of Environmental Psychology, 73(101553), 101553. https://doi.org/10.1016/j.jenvp.2021.101553

Stress. (n.d.). Who.int. https://www.who.int/news-room/questions-and-answers/item/stress

Teaching basic first aid to kids. (2020, December 14). RUN WILD MY CHILD. https://runwildmychild.com/teaching-first-aid/

Teaching teens self-reflection. (2018, February 28). Losangelesteentherapist.com. https://losangelesteentherapist.com/create-a-better-experience-of-life-through-self-reflection/

Teen stress: 10 stress-management skills for teenagers. (2022, March 18). Newport Academy. https://www.newportacademy.com/resources/mental-health/teen-stress-relief/

The University of Queensland. (2021a, October 12). How to build self-confidence in a teenager. Study; The University of Queensland. https://study.uq.edu.au/stories/how-boost-self-confidence-teenager

The University of Queensland. (2021b, November 19). How to teach your teenager emotional intelligence. Study; The University of Queensland. https://study.uq.edu.au/stories/how-teach-your-teenager-emotional-intelligence

Tips for managing conflict. (2016, December 4). Clarke University. https://www.clarke.edu/campus-life/health-wellness/counseling/articles-advice/tips-for-managing-conflict/

VanDuzer, T. (2020, October 23). Time management techniques for teens: The ultimate guide. Student-Tutor Education Blog. https://student-tutor.com/blog/time-management-techniques-for-teens/

Webb, A. (2022, October 26). Research-backed tips to help teens find their purpose. FamilyEducation. https://www.familyeducation.com/teens/values-responsibilities/helping-teens-find-purpose

What is self-care? (n.d.). YoungMinds. https://www.youngminds.org.uk/young-person/coping-with-life/self-care/

Whittington, A. (2020, December 1). 16 survival skills every teenager should learn. Homestead Survival Site. https://homesteadsurvivalsite.com/survival-skills-every-teenager-should-learn/

Women Who Money. (2019, October 18). 10 essential financial lessons for teens. Medishare.com. https://www.medishare.com/blog/10-essential-money-lessons-every-teen-should-learn